The Economic Impact of Christian Missionaries in Zambia

Michael Chanda Chiseni

The Economic Impact of Christian Missionaries in Zambia

A Historical and Long-Term Perspective, 1924–2018

palgrave
macmillan

Michael Chanda Chiseni
Department of Economic History
Lund University
Lund, Sweden

ISBN 978-3-031-65303-2 ISBN 978-3-031-65304-9 (eBook)
https://doi.org/10.1007/978-3-031-65304-9

This Palgrave Macmillan imprint is published by the registered company Springer Nature Switzerland AG.
The registered company address is: Gewerbestrasse 11, 6330 Cham, Switzerland

Paper in this product is recyclable.

Acknowledgements

I am deeply grateful to Jutta Bolt, Jeanne Cilliers, Erik Green, Ellen Hillbom, and Alexandra Lopez Cermeno from Lund University, as well as Felix Meier zu Selhausen from Utrecht University, for their invaluable feedback and contributions to different chapters of this book and my doctoral thesis which has formed the foundation of the material and research presented in this publication. Additionally, I would like to express my heartfelt appreciation to my wife, Tabo Chiseni, for her unwavering patience and support throughout the process of completing this book.

This work was funded by the Knut and Alice Wallenberg Foundation (Grant number KAW 2016.0184).

Contents

About the Author

Michael Chanda Chiseni, PhD holds a doctoral degree in Economic History from Lund University, Department of Economic History. His research focused on investigating the impact of Christian missionary exposure on education and health in Zambia from 1900–2018. With expertise in education and health development in Sub-Saharan Africa, Dr. Michael Chanda Chiseni utilizes micro-econometric and spatial techniques to analyze the long-term factors influencing these areas. Currently, he is a post-doctoral candidate in the Department of Political Science at Gothenburg University, specifically in the Governance and Local Development unit. As part of a project, he aims to comprehend the extent to which African communities are trapped in poverty and explore how the development programs implemented by the World Bank and China can potentially alter these communities' prospects for escaping deprivation. Besides his role at GLD, Michael is a research fellow at the Southern Africa Institute for Policy and Research in Zambia.

List of Figures

1

Introduction

Abstract After independence, there was growing optimism that Sub-Saharan Africa would break free from the shackles of economic stagnation and underdevelopment that had characterized the region for many years. However, the challenges of economic underdevelopment persist, and there are numerous factors that have been invoked to explain Africa's lagging development. Christian missionaries, as colonial actors, have often been overlooked in attempts to comprehend their influence on the development of post-colonial Africa. These missionaries played a crucial role in introducing and providing Western-style education and healthcare in numerous African countries, which are essential components for both human and economic progress. Among these countries, Zambia stood out as one of the most extensively evangelized by Christian missionaries during the twentieth century. Surprisingly, there has been a lack of comprehensive research that explores the impact of Christian missionaries' on Zambia's economic and human development up until now. This chapter serves as an introduction to the key themes addressed in the book.

Keywords Long-term development • Christian missionaries • Health • Education • Sub-Saharan Africa • Zambia

M. Chanda Chiseni, *The Economic Impact of Christian Missionaries in Zambia*,
https://doi.org/10.1007/978-3-031-65304-9_1

Following independence, Sub-Saharan Africa witnessed a surge of optimism for propelling development, and while the region experienced rapid growth in the two decades that ensued, challenges persisted, notably exacerbated by the oil crisis in the 1970s (Barro, 1991). However, by the late 1990s, Africa's growth revival, coupled with improved political and macroeconomic stability, unfolded (Broadberry & Gardner, 2013; Frankema & van Waijenburg, 2018).

Despite these strides, Africa's developmental landscape remains characterized by uneven progress, with a notable lag in critical dimensions such as education and health (United Nations Educational & Organization, 2019; Okoi & Bwawa, 2020). The persistence of gender inequality, particularly in access to education and labor participation, further underscores the multifaceted challenges impeding the region's comprehensive development (Hakura et al., 2016; Bertay et al., 2020).

While numerous factors contribute to Africa's developmental hurdles, the focus on proximate and fundamental sources of development reveals the intricate interplay of geography, institutions, and culture (Szirmai, 2012; Acemoglu et al., 2001; Gallup et al., 1999). The examination of these factors, however, often overlooks the profound influence of colonial actors, including missionaries, on Africa's post-colonial developmental trajectory. This oversight is a critical gap in understanding the divergences in post-colonial development.

Within this context, Zambia emerges as a compelling case study marked by distinct nuances and historical dynamics. The rise of missionary presence in Zambia from the late nineteenth century, intensifying into the mid-twentieth century, marked the nation as one of the most evangelized regions globally (Rotberg, 1965; Beck, 2007). Zambia's enduring Christian identity, with approximately 85 percent of the population identifying as Christian, adds a distinctive layer to its developmental narrative (Phiri, 2019). Even after independence in 1964, Christian missionaries continued to play a pivotal role in providing education and healthcare in Zambia, shaping the country's sociocultural and educational landscape (Gelfand, 1961; Snelson, 1974).

This book aims to fill a critical void in the scholarship by probing into the long-term impacts of missionary exposure on various developmental outcomes in Zambia. Despite the substantial influence of missionaries in Zambia, there is a notable absence of studies delving into this intriguing aspect of the nation's history. As an essential contribution to the growing body of literature on the influence of missionaries in Africa, this book endeavors to illuminate the establishment of education and healthcare by missionaries in Zambia. In doing so, it seeks to establish a meaningful link between the Christian missionary human capital investment legacy and Zambia's contemporary educational and health outcomes, thereby enriching our understanding of the broader forces shaping African development.

Aim and Contributions

The research aims to enhance our comprehension of the enduring influence of the Christian missionary on long-term development. To achieve this objective, the research addresses three overarching questions: (1) What factors influenced the establishment and expansion of missionary activities? (2) What role did missionaries play in shaping the development of education and health as pivotal components of human capital? (3) What are the enduring impacts of missionary investments in human capital on educational attainment, gender inequality, and health?

The earlier literature exploring the consequences of colonialism on Africa's post-colonial development primarily focused on growth disparities based on broad colonial power identities, such as the comparison between former French and British Africa. However, the analysis often overlooked the contributions of various colonial actors. Recent studies have started to scrutinize Africa's development with a renewed focus on previously neglected actors, including Christian missionaries. This research contributes to this evolving discourse by emphasizing the missionaries' role in human capital development and their enduring impact on long-term development.

While many studies examining the contributions of Christian missionaries have taken an all-encompassing approach, encompassing the entire African continent, this book significantly contributes by employing newly collected, precise, localized, and comprehensive data on missionary activities specifically in Zambia. Moreover, while broad Africa-focused studies may reveal general trends, country-specific case studies provide valuable insights into context-specific mechanisms through which missionary exposure influences long-term development. This study stands out as the first to investigate the effects of Christian missionary exposure on long-term educational attainment, gender inequality, and health in Zambia.

Employing time series data encompassing the years 1924 to 1953, this book significantly enhances our comprehension of the historical progression and transformation of education in Zambia. The study delves into the nuances of the historical development and evolution of education, offering valuable insights into Zambia's educational landscape. Moreover, the study also explores the long-term influence of Christian missionaries on educational attainment and gender inequality in education.

Furthermore, this research makes a noteworthy contribution to the discourse on African historical medicine. By utilizing newly collected colonial medical statistics, the study presents a detailed quantitative analysis of Zambia's healthcare history. The research systematically assesses the roles played by the colonial government, medical missionaries, and Africans in shaping the historical development of healthcare in Zambia, providing a nuanced understanding through a quantitative lens. Additionally, the study extends its scrutiny to investigate the long-term impact of Christian missionaries on HIV and related sexual behaviors, further enriching our understanding of the multifaceted influences shaping public health outcomes in Zambia.

Furthermore, this study innovatively addresses a common limitation in existing research on Christian missionaries by utilizing annual missionary data spanning from 1924 to 1953. Unlike studies relying on data from a single point in time, this approach enables a comprehensive analysis of the long-term impacts of Christian missionaries as an ongoing historical process rather than a static event. This temporal granularity allows for a more nuanced understanding, decompressing historical narratives and aligning with the acknowledgement that colonialism was not an isolated event but an endogenous process unfolding over time.

References

Acemoglu, D., Johnson, S., & Robinson, J. A. (2001). The colonial origins of comparative development: An empirical investigation. *American Economic Review, 91*(5), 1369–1401.

Barro, R. J. (1991). Economic growth in a cross-section of countries. *The Quarterly Journal of Economics, 106*(2), 407–443.

Beck, R. B. (2007). All things to all people: Christian missionaries in early Nineteenth-Century South Africa. *Missions, states, and European expansion in Africa*, 11–34.

Bertay, A. C., Dordevic, L., & Sever, C. (2020). *Gender inequality and economic growth: Evidence from industry-level data*. International Monetary Fund.

Broadberry, S., & Gardner, L. (2013). *Africa's growth prospects in a European mirror: A historical perspective*. Citeseer.

Frankema, E., & Van Waijenburg, M. (2018). Africa rising? A historical perspective. *African Affairs, 117*(469), 543–568.

Gallup, J. L., Sachs, J. D., & Mellinger, A. D. (1999). Geography and economic development. *International Regional Science Review, 22*(2), 179–232.

Gelfand, M. (1961). Northern Rhodesia in the Days of the Charter. A Medical and Social Study 1878–1924. In *Northern Rhodesia in the Days of the Charter. A Medical and Social Study 1878–1924*. B. Blackwell.

Hakura, M. D., Hussain, M. M., Newiak, M. M., Thakoor, V., & Yang, M. F. (2016). *Inequality, gender gaps and economic growth: Comparative evidence for sub-Saharan Africa*. International Monetary Fund.

Okoi, O., & Bwawa, T. (2020). How health inequality affect responses to the COVID-19 pandemic in Sub-Saharan Africa. *World development, 135*, 105067.

Phiri, J. M. (2019). How race and law influenced activities in Northern Rhodesia. *African Identities, 17*(3–4), 310–320.

Rotberg, R. I. (1965). *Christian missionaries and the creation of Northern Rhodesia 1880–1924*. Princeton University Press.

Snelson, P. (1974). *Educational development in northern Rhodesia 1883–1945*. Kenneth Kaunda Foundation.

Szirmai, A. (2012). Proximate, intermediate and ultimate causality: Theories and experiences of growth and development. MERIT Working Papers 2012-032, United Nations University—Maastricht Economic and Social Research Institute on Innovation and Technology (MERIT).

United Nations Educational, S., & Organization, C. (2019). *Global education monitoring report 2019: migration, displacement and education: Building bridges, not walls*. UNESCO.

2

Context

Abstract In the twentieth century, Africa became one of the most missionized regions. However, the experiences of the missionaries when settling in Africa varied based on the geographical, cultural, political, and economic context of the various regions. Consequently, studying long-term missionary influence is contingent on understanding the local conditions in which they settled. In this study, I emphasize that case studies provide a better understanding of the context; therefore, this chapter provides a clearer view of Zambia by introducing the geographical, pre-colonial, and colonial context.

Keywords Long-term development • Christian missionaries • Health • Education • Sub-Saharan Africa • Zambia

Geography

Zambia is a landlocked country located at the intersection of Southern, Central, and East Africa. Zambia is endowed with various natural resources, wildlife, forestry, freshwater, and arable land. Zambia is

M. Chanda Chiseni, *The Economic Impact of Christian Missionaries in Zambia*,
https://doi.org/10.1007/978-3-031-65304-9_2

characterized by a tropical climate and experiences two main seasons: the rainy season from November to April and the dry season from May/June to October/November. Several studies have shown that a country's geographical position may affect its economic development (Acemoglu et al., 2002; Bloom et al., 1998; Gallup et al., 1999). In these studies, it is postulated that a region may be endowed poorly with natural resources, unfavorable climate, poor land quality, and a high disease incidence because of its geographical position. Additionally, the geographical position of a country may affect its capacity to access certain technologies and may also affect the prices of certain goods (Venables, 1999). Zambia and other landlocked countries face the challenge of over-dependence on their neighboring countries' transportation infrastructure, which ultimately increases the cost of transporting goods (Faye et al., 2004).

Though Zambia's economy is greatly reliant on the copper mining industry, agriculture is the mainstay of livelihood for the majority of the population in the rural areas. This has typically been the case since the colonial period. The farming practices and types of crops grown in the various regions are contingent on the agro-ecological zone that typifies the region. Figure 2.1 shows Zambia's four main agro-ecological zones: the first is characterized by low rainfall and altitude ranging from 400 to 900 m. Regions in this agro-ecological zone lie along the Lungwa and Zambezi rift valley and are generally hot and dry. The climatic conditions in this zone are mostly suitable for subsistence farming of drought-resistant crops such as sorghum, millet, sesame, and cotton. The area is also prone to flooding and is a habitat of the tsetse fly, limiting cattle rearing in this region. The production of maize, the main staple food in Zambia, is low in this region.

The second agro-ecological zone consists of medium rainfall and has an altitude ranging from 900–1300 m. The main farming areas in Zambia are found within this agro-ecological zone; these are regions on the plateau of Central, Eastern, and Southern Provinces. The zone supports the farming of medium- and long-term crops such as maize, tobacco, cotton,

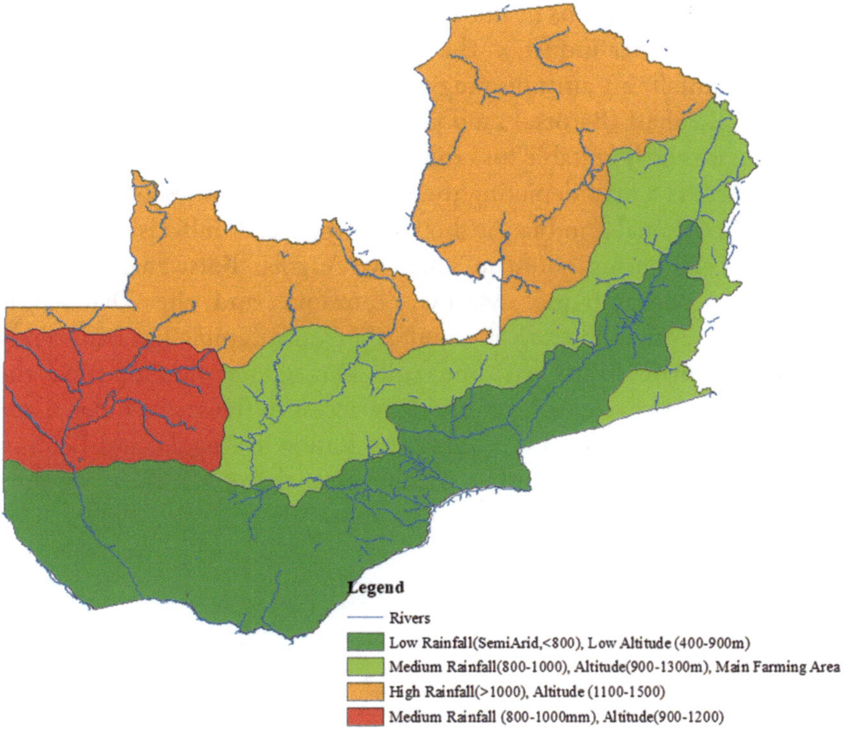

Fig. 2.1 Agroecological zones in Zambia. (Source: Drawn by Author)

wheat, soybean, and groundnuts.[1] Certain parts of this region, especially areas around the Zambezi River, are also suitable for cassava production and fishing. The third agro-ecological zone is characterized by high rainfall, an altitude ranging between 1100 and 1500 m, and comprises some Northern and North-Western provinces. The soils in this zone are moderately fertile. The acidic soils prevalent in some areas of this region are generally suitable for all types of cereals, legumes, tubers, and cassava.

Additionally, because of the high rainfall, other crops cultivated in this region include coffee, sugar cane, rice, and pineapples. The vast forest

[1] Long-term crops are crops that have a lifespan of more than five years, long-term crops have a long waiting period before output can be realized (https://www.toppr.com/ask/en-au/content/concept/crops-in-inida-229988/).

resources and plantations in this region have contributed to the development of the timber industry. The fourth agro-ecological is typified by medium rainfall, an altitude ranging between 900–1200 m and comprises the Kalahari (Barotse) sand plateau and the Zambezi flood plains. This zone is mostly suitable for crops such as tree fruits and vegetables.

Figure 2.2 is a map depicting the location of the mines and historical rail lines in colonial Zambia. As shown in Fig. 2.2, Zambia is surrounded by eight neighboring countries, namely Angola, Botswana, Namibia, Zimbabwe, Mozambique, Malawi, Tanzania, and the Democratic Republic of Congo. Historically, and at present, Zambia has had to rely on other countries for its maritime trade. During the colonial period, the main ports that gave Northern Rhodesia access to the sea included Cape Town in Cape Province, Lobito Bay and Lunda in Angola, and Beira in Mozambique. Noticeable in Fig. 2.2, in colonial Zambia, there was only

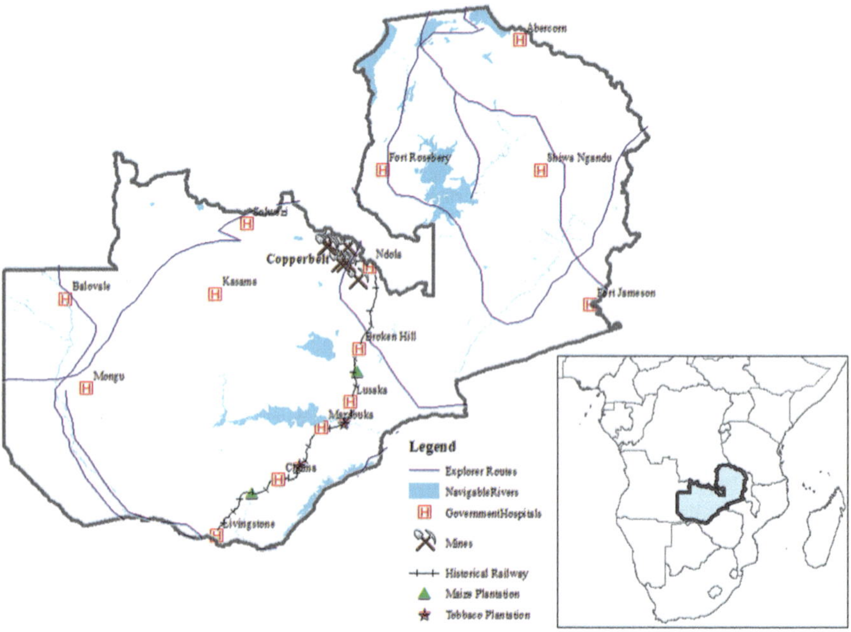

Fig. 2.2 Colonial infrastructure in Northern Rhodesia. (Source: Drawn by author; All maps in this document are produced by the author)

one railway line running from Livingstone to the Copperbelt, where all the copper mines were located. In total, there were five mines located in Lunshya, Rhokana, Mufurila, Nchanga, Chibuluma, and Konkola. From the colonial period until present, Zambia's economy has relied heavily on copper mining. Maize and tobacco plantations were generally located along the railway line—the British colonial government-operated 12 hospitals throughout the colonial period, mostly located in their main administrative centers. The main administration centers are shown in Fig. 2.2. As for the spatial distribution of infrastructure in Fig. 2.2, the colonial infrastructure was mostly developed around the administrative center to cater to the white settlers.

Pre-Colonial Zambia

Before the advent of colonialism, the first European encounter that the Africans had was with the Christian missionaries. The earliest ethnic encounter that the missionaries had was with the Bembas of the Northern province and Lozis of the Barotse plains. Therefore, it is pertinent to understand the pre-colonial context in which missionaries settled. This section also provides context to the pre-colonial ethnic characteristic variables used in some empirical models. For example, in the empirical models, I control for pre-colonial kinship systems, bridal price practice, and agricultural modes. I focus to a greater extent on elaborating these ethnic characteristics for some of the larger tribes, such as the Bembas, Ngoni, and Kololo/Lozi.

The archaeological evidence from Zambia suggests that many of the earliest ethnic societies in Zambia have their origins from the Bantu people of the Great Lakes in East Africa (Wotela, 2010). Figure 2.3 shows the 80 ethnic societies in Zambia, which can be grouped into 13 major ethnic clusters, the Bemba, Lala, Lamba group, Goba group, Kaonde group, Lozi (Kololo), Lunda-Luvale group, Mambwe-Inamwanga group, Nkoya group, Nyanga group, Chewa group, Old Pre-Makololo group, Simaa-Totela group, Swahili group, Tonga-Ila group, Tumbuka group. Roberts (1966) postulates that migration into Zambia began as early as the eleventh century up until the nineteenth century.

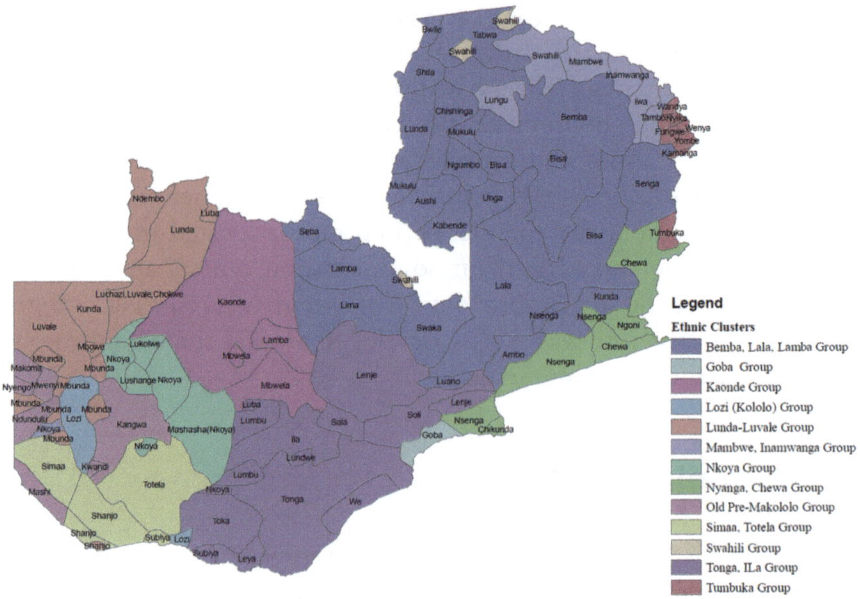

Fig. 2.3 Pre-colonial ethnic boundaries in Zambia. (Source: Drawn by author)

The earliest ethnic clusters to settle in Zambia were the Tonga-Ila group and the Mambwe-Ila group, who settled in Southern-Central and North-Eastern Zambia, respectively. Although there is no sufficient archaeological evidence, these earlier ethnic groups are believed to have migrated into Zambia before the twelfth century (Colson, 1958). The largest ethnic society in the early migration were the Tonga people from the Tonga-Ila group. The following major ethnic group to migrate from the Great Lakes Region through Congo into Zambia is the Bemba; from the Great Lakes region, the Bemba had initially settled among the Luba and Lunda Kingdoms in Congo. The Bemba people ultimately settled in Zambia in the seventeenth century (Richards, 1995). Up to now, the Bemba remain the largest ethnic group in Zambia, comprising about 36 percent of an estimated 17.86 million Zambian population.

Historically not only were the Bembas the largest ethnic group in number, but they are also one of the most important ethnic groups in Zambia (Epstein, 1975). From the time of settlement in Zambia, the

Bembas conquered many ethnic groups in Northern Zambia through military might and prowess. Over a period of 50 years, they had extended their hegemony over this region. The environmental conditions drove the Bemba expansion. Firstly, the Bemba settled in a tsetse fly-infested region; ultimately, it was challenging to raise cattle in this region. Secondly, the soils in the Bembaland were leached and infertile, which made it difficult to grow grain crops (Langworthy, 1972). In Fig. 2.1, the area occupied by the Bemba is typified by high rainfall and an altitude between 1000–1500 meters. To sustain themselves through periods of hunger, the Bembas were forced to raid and conquer the richer tribes for their grains and cattle (Epstein, 1975). Additionally, the Bemba practiced the matrilineal succession tradition, which meant that the ancestral descent was traced through maternal rather than paternal lines. The predominant farming technique that the Bemba practiced is the citemene or the slash and burn system.

More broadly, many ethnic groups in Zambia either trace their ancestry to the Great Lakes region of South Africa; while their customs and norms can be traced back to their region of origin, to a great extent, many of their customs and norms were shaped by the climatic and environmental conditions of the regions where they settled (Brelsford, 1956). For example, the Ngoni and Kololo tribes were cattle herders by virtue of their places of origin. However, the Ngoni people established themselves in the South-eastern region of Zambia; typically, this land is not suitable for herding cattle because it lies in an area with limited grazing land, has a large population of wild animals, and is a breeding ground for tsetse flies (Wotela, 2010). The climatic conditions in this region are suitable for crop cultivation; essentially, crop cultivation is the main mode of farming in this region. Upon settling in the South-eastern region, the Ngoni tribe ultimately shifted from cattle herding to crop cultivation. Moreover, most tribes under the Ngoni umbrella are matrilineal societies, and the strength of their matrilineal land holding culture cannot be questioned (Berge et al., 2014).

In contrast, the Kololo tribe settled in the flood plains in Southwestern Zambia. The environmental conditions of this region were suitable for cattle herding; in essence, the Kololo people, unlike the Ngoni, continued with the tradition of herding cattle (Roberts, 1976). The dominant ethnic group in the region were the Aluyi people. Upon settling in the region in 1838, the Kololos conquered the Aluyi, and they became the Barotse people under the hegemony of the Kololos. The Barotse defeated the Kololos in 1864, and their umbrella name became the Lozi, which referred to the dominant group, the Barotse people and all their subjects. The Lozi people and other tribes in the Zambezi flood plains developed an economy founded on agriculture, fishing, and animal husbandry. In Fig. 2.1, the region occupied by the Lozis is the area in the agro-ecological zone four, typified by an altitude ranging from 900–1200 m, medium rainfall and typically suitable for growing fruits and vegetables. There is no dominant unilineal kinship system among the Lozi. Children can either identify as patrilineal or matrilineal. However, they have a patrilineal bias (Radcliffe-Brown & Forde, 2015).

Pre-Colonial Health and Education System

In Northern Rhodesia, similar to other pre-colonial African societies, the provision of medical care was the responsibility of traditional medicine men (Burke-Gaffney, 1968). The Indigenous people had developed and implemented their own traditional public health care systems (Jennings, 2008; Waite, 1992). Within African societies, many illnesses were traditionally treated within households, utilizing knowledge passed down through generations. It is important to note that not all illnesses in African communities were attributed to spiritual causes, contrary to Western beliefs.

The traditional medicine men, through either chance or enlightenment, had acquired knowledge on how to treat certain illnesses using various leaves, saps, herbs, and roots (Waite, 1992). However, certain illnesses were believed to have spiritual origins. If the traditional healers determined that neglecting certain ancestral rites had caused a particular disease, the individuals involved would make sacrifices to appease the ancestral spirits (Waite, 1992). During the early stages of missionary presence in Africa, the missionaries aimed to "civilize" and "save the souls" of the Africans by replacing many of the African traditional medical practices that they deemed as heathenistic (Aguwa, 2007; Vaughan, 1991).

The education system in Zambia before colonization was firmly grounded in the native cultures and communities, showcasing a comprehensive method of learning that encompassed practical abilities, moral principles, and cultural customs. Education primarily took place in an informal setting, with the community serving as the platform for knowledge dissemination. The elderly members of the society held a pivotal position as custodians of wisdom, employing oral traditions, storytelling, and practical involvement to pass down knowledge to the younger cohorts. This communal education system aimed to equip individuals with the necessary skills and values to fulfill their respective roles within the community, thereby fostering a profound sense of communal responsibility and unity (Kelly, 1999).

In specific Zambian communities, there were specialized establishments that offered more focused educational opportunities. Particularly, within the Bemba society, cultural initiation rituals like the *imbusa* were observed and continue to be practiced to some extent in contemporary Zambia. The *imbusa* serves as a preparatory ceremony for young Bemba women before marriage. The young bride undergoes a period of isolation in a designated house and receives instruction from the *banacimbusa* for a duration ranging from 2 weeks to 3 months leading up to the wedding. Throughout this timeframe, the young bride is imparted with knowledge on how to ensure a "successful" marriage (Kaunda & Reddy, 2013). The *imbusa* traditional ceremony exhibited parallels with the specialized education later offered to girls in missionary schools, specifically the subject of "'home economics'," which aimed to educate young women on the principles of being Christian wives.

The Arrival of Christian Missionaries in Northern Rhodesia

From 1858 to 1863, a Christian revival began in America and spread across the Atlantic to Europe. This revival gave many Christians a new spiritual calling to spread the Gospel of Jesus Christ. This newfound sense of obligation to take the Gospel of Jesus to the ends of the earth inspired many Christians to leave the comfort of their homes to seek and save "the lost world." During this period, many missionary societies were formed, and many of the older missionary societies began to receive support to advance their overseas evangelistic endeavors (Neill, 1964).

In Northern Rhodesia, the first encounter with Europeans by the local people was with the Christian missionaries. David Livingstone, a Scottish explorer, was a key figure in paving the way for missionary activity in Northern Rhodesia. The initial drive behind Livingstone's exploration across the region was his insatiable desire to preach the gospel of Jesus Christ to the unreached people groups of Africa (Rotberg, 1965). However, in 1851 upon reaching the Zambezi River, Livingstone encountered the horrors of the slave trade. At that time, he unwaveringly decided to dedicate his entire life not only to proselytizing the Africans but also to ending the slave trade in Africa (ibid). In his diary, Livingstone wrote:

> You will see what an immense region God in His providence has opened up. If we can enter in and form a settlement, we shall be able to put a stop to the slave trade in that quarter. Providence seems to call me to the regions beyond. (As quoted in Rotberg, 1965, p. 23)

Livingstone's first visit to the Barotseland in 1853 paved the way for French and British missionaries in Northern Rhodesia (Rotberg, 1965). Upon arrival, the prominent proselytization strategies among the Christian missionaries included the provision of Western-styled education and health care. However, evangelism through the provision of formal education was initially a Protestant strategy since a fundamental impetus for the Protestants was to enable their converts to read the Bible in their languages (Woodberry, 2004).

Christian Missionaries and Education in Northern Rhodesia

In 1883, a Scottish missionary, Fredrick Stanley Arnot, established the first missionary school in Northern Rhodesia among the Lozi people in the Barotse region (Kelly, 1999; Snelson, 1974). The school closed within a very short period. The school's failure was due to the non-conformity of the local people to the idea of regularly attending school. Francis Coillard of the Paris Evangelical Mission later opened another school in the Barotse expanse in 1886 (Snelson, 1974). Though Coillard faced similar challenges to Arnot, these were overcome when Coillard began to receive support from Chief Lewanika of the Lozi people. Lewanika's influence led to a proliferation in school enrolments in the region, such that even the commoners had an equal opportunity to access missionary education.

After settling in Northern Rhodesia, like the Paris Evangelical Mission, most mission societies first established schools before establishing health care facilities. The London Mission Society (LMS) established its first school in 1889 at Fwambo in Northern Zambia among the Bemba people. Despite being understaffed and in short of resources, they successfully expanded their educational outreach in Northern Zambia, such that by 1925 they had opened about 240 schools with about 12,000 enrolled pupils and 20 European teachers engaged in education (Snelson, 1974). Their greatest contribution to the development of education in Northern Rhodesia was their active involvement in improving female education. They are recorded as the first Protestant mission society to send a female missionary, Mabel Shaw, to establish a girl's boarding school at Mbereshi in 1915 (Snelson, 1974; Ragsdale, 1986). Mabel Shaw's success is said to have encouraged other Protestant missionary societies to send female missionaries for a similar cause.

The Primitive Methodist society reached Northern Rhodesia in 1893 and settled among the Ba-Ila people at Nkala. They established their first school with about 25 pupils at Nkala in 1895. However, the Primitive Methodists faced numerous challenges with regard to establishing schools among the Ila; parents demanded gifts before they would send their children to school, child marriage robbed schools of their girl pupils, and because children played an imperative role in the village economy, school attendance was very poor for most of the year. The attitude towards school nonetheless changed when Chief Lewanika of the Lozi stressed the importance of missionary education to the Ila Chiefs. In a letter to Reverend W. Chapman, Lewanika is chronicled to have said that he advised every Ila Chief that visited him to open a school in their district (Snelson, 1974; Ragsdale, 1986). Lewanika's intervention propelled the educational success of the Primitive Methodist among the Ila People, such that by 1925, the society was operating 58 schools, with an estimated total of about 2000 children enrolled in the schools. The society contributed greatly to the development of education in Northern Rhodesia. They were the first mission society to operate a formal teacher training college at Kafue under the leadership of Reverend John Fell.

The United Free Church of Scotland extended their work from Nyasaland into North-Eastern Rhodesia in 1895, setting up a mission station at Mwenzo. After establishing a mission station, they established their first school; however, their educational progress was slow because of understaffing. In 1900, Dr James Chisholm, a medical missionary, took over the running of the Mwenzo mission station. Soon after, Dr Chisholm and his wife, Catherine MacGailvary, began to train Indigenous teacher-evangelists to assist them in their educational and proselytization mission (Snelson, 1974). Dr Chisholm and Catherine MacGailvary made great strides such that by 1904, the society, through the assistance of the autochthonous teacher-evangelists, had established about 32 schools with 1000 pupils enrolled.

Under the auspices of the Catholic Church, the White Fathers began their work in Northern Zambia among the Bemba people at Kayambi in 1895. By 1896, the White Fathers had opened their first school at Kayambi with only 14 boys in attendance. Despite such a humble beginning, by 1897, they had 235 children enrolled at the school, many of whom boarded at the school (Snelson, 1974). Like the Protestant missionaries, the White Fathers also had a challenge regarding pupils' irregular attendance at school. Because the White Fathers were financially resourced, they could afford to pay the children a penny a day for regular attendance.

In 1902, the White Sisters arrived at Chilubula to assist the White Fathers' evangelistic and educational mission. The White Sisters established a literacy class to train teacher-evangelists a few years later. By 1911, about 300 men were trained as teacher-evangelists. The training of teacher-evangelists greatly increased the number of village schools run by the White Fathers (Carmody, 1999). The White Fathers had unprecedented success in opening village schools, so that, by 1925, they had established more than 500 village schools with about 25,000 children in enrolment; Snelson (1974) avers that the majority of these schools were in the Eastern province of Northern Rhodesia where the White Fathers were in a battle for converts with the Dutch Reformed Church.

The Dutch Reformed Church (DRC) was also considered an influential force in the early development of education in Northern Rhodesia. They began their education work in 1898 when they established their first mission station at Magwero in the Eastern province (Rotberg, 1965). The society brought several African teacher-evangelists trained in Nyasaland to assist them with their evangelistic and educational work in Northern Rhodesia (Snelson, 1974). With the help of the African teacher-evangelists, the Dutch Reformed Society opened many village schools. Under the Northern Rhodesian administrator R. Codrington, a "Sphere of Influence" policy was enacted to settle the conflicts among various societies for territories. The policy entailed that whenever a mission society opened a school in an area, they could claim exclusive rights over the population of that specific area (Carmody, 1999). However, the White Fathers did not abide by this policy; ultimately, they conflicted with the London Mission and Livingstonia Mission in the Northern province of Northern Rhodesia and the Dutch Reformed Church in Northern Eastern Rhodesia (Rotberg, 1965). The competition for turf with the White Fathers gave the Dutch Reformed Church impetus to establish many village schools. The DRC's educational work was a great success, such that, by 1925, they had established about 250 schools with about 25,000 pupils enrolled (Snelson, 1974).

The educational work of the above-mentioned early missionary societies made it possible for subsequent Christian missionaries to enter the educational scene. By 1900, about seven mission societies were operating only a few schools across the Northern Rhodesian expanse (Rotberg, 1965).

In the years that followed, there was a tremendous proliferation in mission activity throughout the region, such that, in 1946, there existed approximately 21 mission societies running 1061 schools. During the early establishment of mission education in Northern Rhodesia, missionaries experienced similar challenges. Firstly, as previously mentioned, children played an imperative role in the village economy. Consequently, the schools competed for the children's attention with the various vocational demands (Rotberg, 1965). The children were required to work in the fields during the planting and harvesting seasons. Fundamentally, schools were considered places to go when there was no immediate need for the children in the village economy (Snelson, 1974). Though the missionaries were enthusiastic about providing formal education, the Africans did not deem it necessary until the 1930s and 1940s, when employment opportunities that required a degree of formal education began to open up.

Christian Missionaries and health care in Northern Rhodesia

The educational work of the missionaries preceded health care provision in Northern Rhodesia, more so because healthcare required more resource investment than education. Although the literature on the work of the medical missionaries in Northern Rhodesia is scanty, the available literature emphasizes that Christian missionaries were the initiators and main providers of Western-style health care in Northern Rhodesia (Gann, 1968, 1969; Gelfand, 1961; Walima T Kalusa, 2007). Upon arrival in Northern Rhodesia, missionaries viewed the locals as oppressed by tropical diseases and culturally backward. The missionaries, therefore, believed that they possessed a superior healing system to cure the ills of the locals and the gospel to cure their backwardness (Kalusa, 2014). In the early stages of missionary establishment in Northern Rhodesia, the missionaries had limited human and financial resources to set up fully-fledged medical facilities (Gelfand, 1961). The missionaries established rudimentary healthcare services alongside their homes. These medical dispensaries were mostly used to bandage wounds and dispense medicine (Kalusa, 2003).

Although the pioneer missionaries in the initial stages only provided rudimentary medical services, some of the basic medical procedures performed by the missionaries appeared miraculous to the locals. The Africans were initially opposed to receiving treatment from the missionary dispensaries. Still, as the missionaries demonstrated their ability to alleviate pain and heal the sick, they ultimately gained a reputation among the Africans (Gelfand, 1961). In 1898, Chief Mwamba, a Bemba chief, fell ill, and Father Dupont of the White Father Catholic order was called upon to cure his ailment. After curing the illness that had struck Chief Mwamba, Father Dupont developed a significant level of trust with the Chief to the extent that Chief Mwamba wanted to name Dupont the next heir to his throne, but Father Dupont rejected this offer (Rotberg, 1965).

The efficacy of missionary medicine in curing various illnesses triggered a proliferation in African attendances to missionary medical facilities. The missionaries soon realized that their rudimentary medical services could not meet the medical demands of the locals, and there was a dire need to broaden the scope of their medical services. The provision of medical services had proved to be a powerful evangelizing tool, missionaries began to implore their home churches to send more financial resources and ordained doctors to aid the expansion of their medical work. Though discussions were initiated, it took many years for missionaries to receive the help they requested from the various missionary societies (Rotberg, 1965). The delay was partly because good missionary doctors were difficult to find and expensive to maintain. When available, the doctors were sent to China and India, where the societies were already well-established. Before 1910, only the London Mission Society (LMS), Livingstonia Mission, and Brethren in Christ Mission society had qualified missionary doctors at their main medical centers in Northern Rhodesia. In the years that followed, other missionary societies began to likewise send qualified medical missionary doctors (Gann, 1969).

Colonial Period

The Beginning of Mining Exploration in Northern Rhodesia by the British South African Company

The initial impetus of the British South African company was to gain mining rights in the Katanga region. Still, after a failed attempt due to opposition by rivals financed by King Leopold II of Belgium, they settled and searched for minerals in Northern Rhodesia. The occupation of Northern Rhodesia by the British South African Company was made possible through Francis Coillard, a Paris Evangelical Mission Priest with

King Lewanika. During his time in Barotse land, the region experienced many tribal tensions (Gann, 1969). Coillard was convinced that the Lozi people were incapable of governing themselves. To Coillard, establishing a formal government would prevent further tribal unrest in Barotseland and bring about systematic developments in Lewanika's kingdom (Gann, 1969). Ultimately, Coillard persuaded Lewanika that seeking British Protection would prevent civil wars and hinder the Ndebele from attacking. Chief Kgama, who had been a personal adviser to Lewanika, reinforced Coillard's advice to the Lozi Chief, and he was quoted to have told Lewanika that:

> I have the people of the great Queen with me, and I am glad to have them. I live in peace with them and I have no fear of the Matabele or the Boers any longer attacking me. (As quoted in Snelson, 1974)

In 1890, the British South African Company (BSAC) sent a representative, Frank Eliot Lochner, to obtain Lewanika's signature on a treaty that the Company had drafted. After several negotiations, Coillard finally convinced the Chief to sign the treaty. Essentially, if it were not for the intervention of Coillard, the signing of the treaty would have taken long and ultimately, British rule in North-Western Rhodesia would have been less peacefully with much bloodshed. The treaty entailed that the Company would pay an annual subsidy to the Lozi Kingdom and offer them protection. The treaty endowed the British South African Company with the exclusive rights to settle in Barotseland, conduct mineral exploitation, and eventually obtain significant control over North-Western Rhodesia (Rotberg, 1965). Exploiting the loopholes in the treaty, the Company also took claim of the mineral-rich Copperbelt in Northern Rhodesia.

In the same year, the BSAC had also endeavored to sign treaties with Chief Mpeseni of the Ngoni in North-Eastern Rhodesia and Chief Chitimukulu, the paramount chief in the Bembaland; the attempts to sign treaties in this region were futile. In 1890, the BSAC managed to sign another treaty with Chief Kazembe in Luapula district, the area in the west of the Northern province of Zambia, as seen in Fig. A3. The successful signing of the various treaties ultimately gave the Company mineral rights. During the Company's rule in Northern Rhodesia, the Company introduced taxation on the local people to increase their fiscal capacity. As part of the treaty, the British South African Company had promised to develop public infrastructures such as schools and hospitals. However, they failed to follow through on their promise (Gann, 1969).

A great deal of the Company's revenue was also generated from land sales, selling investment shares, and mining royalties. It is worth noting that the Company easily enforced taxation among people with a strong tribal organization, including the Bemba, Ngoni, and Kazembe people. Although the Company was collecting taxes and was raising revenue from mining royalties and the sale of land, the Company hardly invested in developing the public infrastructures of Northern Rhodesia. Throughout the Company's rule, Northern Rhodesia was classified as a mono-crop and mono-mineral economy (Gann, 1969). The Company had restricted the autochthonous farmers; the Indigenous farmers were to a great extent only allowed to farm for subsistence purposes. The white settlers were awarded the exclusive right to sell farm produce for profit or cash crops. The Africans were prevented from growing cash crops because the colonial administration feared that their "primitive" agricultural practices would spread disease, ultimately affecting their plantations (Krishna & Mwansa, 2020).

The British South African Company ultimately had little involvement in developing education in Northern Rhodesia; even though they formally conferred the responsibility of providing education to the missionaries, they did not fund them. Apart from the White Fathers, who received a great deal of financial and human resource support from abroad, most missionary societies lacked the financial and human capacity to provide quality education (Carmody, 1999). Additionally, during the British South African Company rule, the Company barely supported the medical missionaries' work, with a significant amount of the support coming instead from the societies (Gelfand, 1961). The lack of involvement in the provision of public goods by the Company made the missionaries the key providers of health and education among the African population. In the following section, I also accentuate their key involvement in the provision of public goods during the rule of the British colonial administration.

The British Colonial Government in Northern Rhodesia

Following the increase in European white settlers in Northern Rhodesia, the white settler population in Northern Rhodesia began to demand a political voice in the administration of Northern Rhodesia. In addition to the growing pressure from the white settler population, the administration of Northern Rhodesia became a financial burden for the British South African Company. The British South African Company saw this as an opportunity to rid themselves of the financial burden that came with the administrative responsibility of governing Northern Rhodesia (Slinn, 1971). By 1920, negotiations began to hand over the administrative responsibility of Northern Rhodesia to the British colonial government. Following the Devonshire Agreement in 1923, the Company fully handed over the administration obligation of Northern Rhodesia to the colonial government in April 1924 (Frederiksen, 2010). The African population in 1924 was estimated to be at 1.1 million, and the European population stood at 4182 (Colonial Office, 1924). Unlike in the neighboring Southern Rhodesia, where white settlement began with violent conquest then followed by negotiations, in Northern Rhodesia, as earlier indicated, the British South African Company peacefully signed a concession that gave them mineral and administration rights in the territory with the help of the missionaries. By 1964 constituted about 5 percent of the population south of the Sahara, with 80 percent of the white settler population concentrated in South Africa, Southern Rhodesia, and Northern Rhodesia. Though the white settlers constituted the ethnic minority in the colonies, they justified their occupation and extended their hegemony because they brought with them "Western civilization" (Kuper, 1964).

The British colonial government inherited a country with an underdeveloped public service sector. However, unlike the Company, the British colonial government began to give grants to Christian missionaries for education and health provision for the African population (Gelfand, 1961). The British colonial government became greatly involved in developing the African education system. They began by establishing a subdepartment of African Education under the Department of African

Affairs in 1925 (Snelson, 1974). In 1927, the African Education Department enacted the Native School Code. The code defined a school as "a class or assembly for the teaching or instruction of locals, whether held in a building or not, conducted for not less than 120 days in a year and in which instructions are based on a code approved by the Director of African Education and Advisory Board on African Education" (Carmody, 1999, p. 11). Any school that did not meet the criteria stipulated by the Native School Code was considered a sub-school.

Additionally, the British government only funded schools that fell within the definition of a school. Numerous schools established by the mission societies failed to meet the conditions outlined in the code, which led to a significant reduction in the number of mission schools recognized as formal schools (Snelson, 1974). For example, after the enactment of the Native School Code, only 17 of the 530 White Fathers' schools were considered to be schools, and the African Education Department considered only 8 out of 545 schools of the Dutch Reformed Church as schools (ibid.).

Moreover, after taking over the administration of Northern Rhodesia from the British South African Company, the British colonial government began to fund missionaries for their medical work among the local people. In the early years, the British colonial government was resource-constrained; therefore, their financial support to the missionaries was greatly limited (Gann, 1969). In the 1933 Northern Rhodesian medical report, it was indicated that the government spent 2950 pounds in aid to all missionary societies that actively provided medical services to the autochthonous population; this amounted to about 5 percent of the total health expenditure.[2] In the years that followed, the grant offered to the missionaries did not increase significantly; in 1937, the government spent an estimated 3165 pounds on medical grants to the missionaries and 3781 pounds in 1939 which was an average of about 4.5 percent of the total health expenditure (Medical Report, 1939).

The British colonial government had also entrusted the missionaries with the responsibility of training African medical orderlies. Many of the

[2] £2,950 in 1933 is equivalent in purchasing power to about £216,573.12 today, an increase of £213,623.12 over 88 years (www.in2013dollars.com/uk/inflation).

African medical staff that worked in the African government hospital were trained by the missionaries (Gelfand, 1961). The medical reports do not give us the full scope of the number of Africans that worked in both the missionary and African government hospitals; they only include the number of African medical staff that worked in the African colonial hospitals. The medical reports show that, by 1933, about 250 African medical staff were employed in the British colonial government African hospitals. By 1955, an estimated 1200 African staff were employed in the African colonial hospitals. The African medical staff included microscopists, vaccinators, malaria control boys, orderlies, and sleeping sickness guards (Medical Report, 1938).

Throughout the colonial period, Christian missionaries continued to be the main providers of medical services among the African population. In 1933, the medical reports show that the missionaries had established 27 hospitals across the territory; by 1952, the various missionary societies ran about 85 hospitals in Northern Rhodesia. The British government had only established 12 African hospitals throughout the colonial period. They relied greatly on the missionary to provide various medical services to the majority of the African populations. In 1946, the Chief medical doctor in the territory reported:

> There is a great volume of medical activity by the missionary societies, and these activities are more widely spread over the territory than those of the Health Department itself. The main activities of missions which are related to the work of the Health Department are in the domain of curative medicine. However, missionary schools all include instruction in simple hygiene in their curriculum. (Medical Report, 1946)

References

Acemoglu, D., Johnson, S., & Robinson, J. A. (2002). Reversal of fortune: Geography and Institutions in the making of the Modern World Income Distribution. *The Quarterly Journal of Economics, 117*(4), 1231–1294.

Aguwa, J. C. U. (2007). Mission, colonialism, and the supplanting of African religious and medical practices. *Missions, States, and European Expansion in Africa*, 127–145.

Berge, E., Kambewa, D., Munthali, A., & Wiig, H. (2014). Lineage and land reforms in Malawi: Do matrilineal and patrilineal landholding systems represent a problem for land reforms in Malawi? *Land Use Policy, 41*, 61–69.

Bloom, D. E., Sachs, J. D., Collier, P., & Udry, C. (1998). Geography, demography, and economic growth in Africa. *Brookings Papers on Economic Activity, 1998*(2), 207–295.

Brelsford, W. (1956). *The Tribes of Northern*. Rhodesia (Lusaka).

Burke-Gaffney, H. O. D. (1968). The history of medicine in the African countries. *Medical History, 12*(1), 31–41.

Carmody, B. (1999). *Education in Zambia: Catholic perspectives*. Bookworld Publication.

Colonial Office. (1924). *Blue book for Northern Rhodesia*. His Majesty's Stationery Office.

Colson, E. (1958). *Marriage & the family among the plateau Tonga of Northern Rhodesia*. Manchester University Press.

Epstein, A. L. (1975). Military organization and the pre-colonial polity of the Bemba of Zambia. *Man, 10*, 199–217.

Faye, M. L., McArthur, J. W., Sachs, J. D., & Snow, T. (2004). The challenges facing landlocked developing countries. *Journal of Human Development, 5*(1), 31–68.

Gallup, J. L., Sachs, J. D., & Mellinger, A. D. (1999). Geography and economic development. *International Regional Science Review, 22*(2), 179–232.

Gann, L. H. (1968). *The birth of a plural society: The development of Northern Rhodesia under the British South Africa Company, 1894–1914*. Manchester University Press.

Gann, L. H. (1969). *A history of Northern Rhodesia: Early days to 1953*. Humanities Press.

Gelfand, M. (1961). Northern Rhodesia in the Days of the Charter. A Medical and Social Study 1878–1924. In *Northern Rhodesia in the Days of the Charter. A Medical and Social Study 1878–1924*. B. Blackwell.

Jennings, M. (2008). 'Healing of bodies, salvation of souls': Missionary medicine in colonial Tanganyika, 1870s–1939. *Journal of Religion in Africa, 38*(1), 27–56.

Kalusa, W. T. (2003). *Disease and the remaking of missionary medicine in colonial northwestern Zambia: A case study of Mwinilunga district, 1902–1964*.

Kalusa, W. T. (2007). Language, medical auxiliaries, and the re-interpretation of Missionary Medicine in Colonial Mwinilunga, Zambia, 1922–51. *Journal of Eastern African Studies, 1*(1), 57–78.

Kalusa, W. T. (2014). Missionaries, African patients, and negotiating missionary medicine at Kalene Hospital, Zambia, 1906–1935. *Journal of Southern African Studies, 40*(2), 283–294.
Kaunda, M., & Reddy, S. (2013). Pedagogies of subservience? A feminist exploration of the Institution of Imbusa among the Bemba. *Journal of Gender and Religion in Africa, 19*(2), 119–139.
Kelly, M. J. (1999). *The origins and Developments of Education in Zambia from Pre-Colonial Time to 1996: A Book of Notes and Readings*. Image Publishers.
Krishna, K., & Mwansa, D. (2020). Colonial economy adversely impacted on Zambian and Indian women. *International Journal of Latest Research in Humanities and Social Science (IJLRHSS), 3*(08).
Kuper, H. (1964). The colonial situation in Southern Africa. *The Journal of Modern African Studies, 2*(2), 149–164.
Langworthy, H. (1972). Pre-Colonial Kingdoms and Tribal Migrations, AD 1500–1900. In D. Davies (Ed.), *Zambia in maps* (p. 12). New York: Africana.
Medical Report, N. R. (1938). *Medical Report on Health and Sanitary Conditions for the Year 1938.*
Medical Report, N. R. (1939). *Medical Report on Health and Sanitary Conditions for the Year 1939.*
Medical Report, N. R. (1946). *Medical Report on Health and Sanitary Conditions for the Year 1946.*
Neill, S. (1964). *A history of Christian Missions*. Grand Rapids: Wm. B. Eerdmans Publishing Company.
Radcliffe-Brown, A. R., & Forde, D. (2015). *African systems of kinship and marriage*. Routledge.
Ragsdale, J. P. (1986). *Protestant mission education in Zambia, 1880–1954*. Susquehanna University Press.
Richards, A. I. (1995). *Land, labour and diet in Northern Rhodesia: An economic study of the Bemba tribe*. LIT Verlag Münster.
Roberts, A. (1966). Migrations from the Congo. *Short History of Zambia, Nairobi*, 101–120.
Roberts, A. (1976). *A history of Zambia*. Heinemann Educational Publishers.
Rotberg, R. I. (1965). *Christian missionaries and the creation of Northern Rhodesia 1880–1924*. Princeton University Press.
Slinn, P. (1971). Commercial concessions and politics during the colonial period: The role of the British South Africa Company in Northern Rhodesia 1890–1964. *African Affairs, 70*(281), 365–384.
Snelson, P. (1974). *Educational development in Northern Rhodesia 1883–1945.*

Vaughan, M. (1991). *Curing their ills: Colonial power and African illness*. Stanford University Press.

Venables, A. J. (1999). But why does geography matter, and which geography matters? *International Regional Science Review, 22*(2), 238–241.

Waite, G. (1992). Public Health in Precolonial East-Central Africa. In *The Social Basis of Health and Healing in Africa*, 212–231.

Woodberry, R. D. (2004). *The shadow of empire: Christian missions, colonial policy, and democracy in postcolonial societies*. University of North Carolina at Chapel Hill Manuscript.

Wotela, K. (2010). Deriving ethno-geographical clusters for comparing ethnic differentials in Zambia. *World Cultures eJournal, 17*(2), 1–30.

3

Developmental Challenges in the Post-Independence Era

Abstract This book aims to explore the enduring influence of Christian missionaries in Zambia over the long term. Considering the longitudinal nature of this study, a crucial aspect is to provide an overview of Zambia's economic development since gaining independence. In this chapter, the focus is on accentuating Zambia's journey in the post-independence era, detailing significant economic shifts, and examining challenges encountered in the education and health sectors.

Keywords Long-term development • Christian missionaries • Health • Education • Sub-Saharan Africa • Zambia

Zambia gained its independence on the 24th of October 1964. The population of Zambia was estimated to be at 3.4 million at independence and has since grown to an estimated 18.3 million in 2020 (World Bank, 2019). After independence, Zambia had inherited a thriving copper economy and had the fourth-highest GDP per capita in Africa. After independence, Zambia continued to rely greatly on the mining sector (Whitworth, 2015). The mining sector accounted for 49.6 percent of

M. Chanda Chiseni, *The Economic Impact of Christian Missionaries in Zambia*,
https://doi.org/10.1007/978-3-031-65304-9_3

Zambia's total GDP (Jenkin, 2018). Additionally, at independence, copper constituted 93% of Zambia's export and accounted for 71% of the government revenue. In essence, the copper industry determined Zambia's economic trajectory (Whitworth, 2015). A decade after independence, the world copper prices fell significantly; it is estimated that between 1974 and 1975, copper prices fell by 40 percent while import prices increased by 16 percent annually (Shaw, 1982).

The falling copper prices reduced government revenues and exacerbated the fiscal deficits (Chirwa and Odhiambo, 2017). To finance government expenditure, the Zambian government increased taxes which led to an increase in inflation; between 1975 and 1980, the inflation rate increased from 8 percent per annum to 16 percent per annum (Andersson et al., 2000). In 1978, the International Monetary Fund (IMF) assisted the Zambian government financially to restore Zambia's balance of payments and reduce the inflation rate. During this period, a short-lived increase in copper prices enabled the Zambian government to meet the conditions stipulated in the IMF Action Programme, which had come at the expense of partially losing economic policy autonomy (Andersson et al., 2000). In 1983, challenges related to maintaining the momentum from the 1978 IMF Action Programme led to the adoption of a new comprehensive structural adjustment program. The new structural adjustment program aimed to strengthen production incentives, foster economic growth, and diversify the export industry (Andersson & Kayizzi-Mugerwa, 1989).

Additionally, as part of this new program, the Zambian government was required to deregulate the interest rates and prices and mandated to reduce tariffs. Moreover, under this program, the tax systems, trade industry, and the parastatals were to go through a reformation process (Andersson et al., 2000). The implementation of the new structural adjustment program did not produce the intended results; the Zambian economy further dwindled into a quagmire, which ultimately led to the abandonment of the adjustment by the Zambian government in 1987. The Zambian government went from liberalized economy to a command and control economy. Which entailed that adjustment and economic growth were to occur through the country's resources (Andersson & Kayizzi-Mugerwa, 1989).

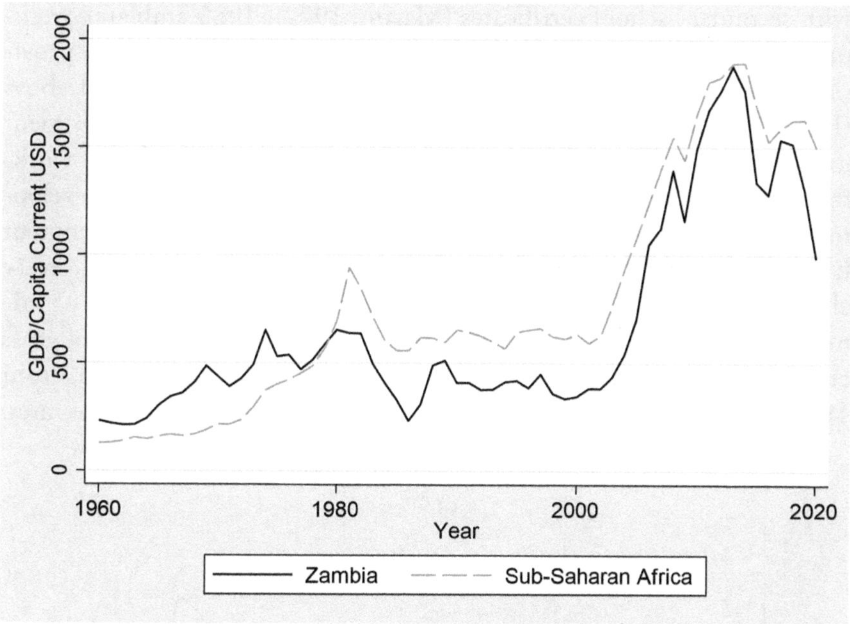

Fig. 3.1 Evolution of GDP per capita in Zambia and Sub-Saharan Africa 1960–2019. (Source: World Bank ("Figure caption (from [x.y], licensed under CC-BY 4.0)"))

Additionally, in the years that followed independence, the GDP per capita remained relatively low. As shown in Fig. 3.1, for much of the period between 1960 to about 2003, the GDP per capita remained below 500 USD. It was only after 2000 when Zambia experienced a sharp increase in the GDP per capita; there was a sustained increase from 480 USD in 2000 to about 1900 USD in 2017. Additionally, the GDP per capita in Zambia followed a similar trajectory as the average of Sub-Saharan Africa.

Education in the Post-Independence Era

At independence, Zambia was faced with the challenge of having an uneducated workforce; it is estimated that in 1963, there were fewer than a hundred Zambians with a university degree and less than 1000 Africans with secondary school certificates (Martin, 1972). The Zambian government had also inherited a gender unequal education because the provision of education by Christian missionaries was biased towards boys (Kelly, 1999). Essentially, after independence, the Zambian government invested heftily in education in an attempt to increase its skilled workforce and close the gender gap in education. Moreover, in the development plan adopted by the government at independence, the government had planned to expand its education system such that, by 1970, every child of school-going age would have attained at least four years of primary education (Kelly, 1999). Figure 3.2 shows the primary school gross enrolment rates from 1970 to 2017 in Zambia. As can be seen, from 1970, there was a steady increase in primary school gross enrolment rates.

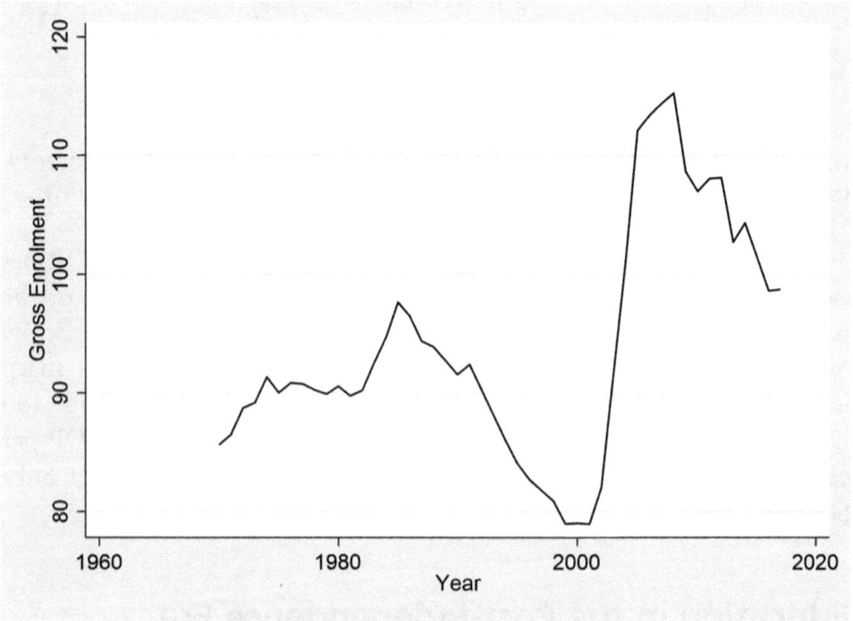

Fig. 3.2 Primary school gross enrolment in Zambia 1970–2017. (Source: World Bank ("Figure caption (from [x.y], licensed under CC-BY 4.0)"); Around 2001, there is a pronounced spike in gross enrolment, the literature does not document any significant event during this period that may have led to this spike. The spike could be as a result of data mis-reporting)

The increase may have responded to the schooling expansionary policy adopted in the post-independence era.

Despite the efforts made by the post-independence government to increase the quality and access to education, to date, there remain huge disparities in education with regards to gender, region, and social class (UNESCO, 2015). Approximately about 27 percent of females and 18 percent of males in rural areas have not had any access to schooling (Masaiti & Chita, 2014). Additionally, females are more likely to drop out of school after their first year of primary schooling relative to males (Nkosha & Mwanza, 2009). Various studies have shown that education for girls is also linked to broader societal benefits such as later marriage, lower fertility, better health care, and improved education for their children (Klasen, 2002; Lloyd et al., 2000; World Bank, 2017). Other studies have shown that female education empowers women to have significant autonomy over their sexuality and is linked to lower HIV infection among females (Alsan & Cutler, 2013; Brent, 2006).

Healthcare in the Post-Independence Era

In the post-independence era, the Zambian government had inherited an unbalanced public health system. The British colonial government had not invested greatly in developing the public health system but rather depended on the Christian missionaries to meet the health care demands of the majority of the local population in the rural areas. The public health facilities were unevenly distributed at independence, with most well-developed health centers located in administrative and principal towns. The new government was faced with the challenge of redressing the public health care inequalities that had characterized the region during the colonial era. In the years that followed independence, the Zambian government invested heftily in developing the public health care system; for example, in 1964, the Zambian government-operated 19 hospitals across Zambia (Freund, 1986). By 1990, there were 42 government hospitals. The new government also began to expand the rural health care facilities; between 1964 and 1990, the rural health facilities increased from 187 to 661 (Kamwanga et al., 1999).

The Zambian health care system has undergone several transformation stages; for example, in the early 1980s, the Zambian government decentralized the health care system, which entailed that the responsibility of managing health care in the various districts in Zambia was entrusted to the district health boards and hospitals rather than the Ministry of Health. Additionally, in a bid to continue expanding the health care system during times of economic austerity, the Zambian government introduced primary health care fees in the 1990s. Eventually, the introduction of health care fees has created barriers to access for poor people (Hjortsberg & Mwikisa, 2002). In 2006, the Zambian government abolished the health care user fees (Masiye et al., 2008). Though remarkable progress has been made since independence, the health care system in Zambia still faces a few challenges: (1) there are still huge disparities in access to health. It is estimated that only 46 percent of the population lives within a 5 km radius of a health facility. At the same time, the greater majority travel a distance of about 50 km to have access to a health facility. (2) There is a shortage of trained health workers, which has led to some facilities being operated by unqualified workers (ACCA, 2013).

The fractured health system in Zambia has also diminished its capacity to deal with the HIV epidemic. A report by ARHAP (2006) indicates that Zambia is among the Southern African countries most hard hit by the HIV epidemic. It is estimated that about 20 percent of adult deaths are attributed to HIV. The prevalence among young people stands at 6.6 percent, with HIV prevalence higher among females than males (Nakazwe et al., 2019).

This section has highlighted that Zambia inherited an uneven education and health sector at independence; however, since independence, Zambia has made considerable strides in developing education and health care. Though significant progress has been made, education and health are still unequally distributed and underdeveloped; therefore, the fundamental impetus of this study is to understand how the historical Christian missionary investments in education and health have shaped current educational and health outcomes in Zambia.

References

ACCA. (2013). *Key health challenges for Zambia.* Retrieved from Lusaka.

Alsan, M. M., & Cutler, D. M. (2013). Girls' education and HIV risk: Evidence from Uganda. *Journal of Health Economics, 32*(5), 863–872.

Andersson, P.-Å., Bigsten, A., & Persson, H. (2000). *Foreign aid, debt, and growth in Zambia.* Nordic Africa Institute.

Andersson, P.-Å., & Kayizzi-Mugerwa, S. (1989). *Mineral dependence, goal attainment and equity: Zambia's experience with structural adjustment in the 1980s.* Swedish International Development Authority.

ARHAP. (2006). *Mapping, understanding, translating and engaging religious health assets in Zambia and Lesotho.*

Brent, R. J. (2006). Does female education prevent the spread of HIV-AIDS in Sub-Saharan Africa? *Applied Economics, 38*(5), 491–503.

Chirwa, T. G., & Odhiambo, N. M. (2017). Macroeconomic policy reform and economic growth in Zambia. *Euroeconomica, 35*(2), 156–166.

Freund, P. J. (1986). Health care in a declining economy: The case of Zambia. *Social Science & Medicine, 23*(9), 875–888.

Hjortsberg, C., & Mwikisa, C. (2002). Cost of access to health services in Zambia. *Health Policy and Planning, 17*(1), 71–77.

Jenkin, S. (2018). *Foreign investment in agricultural development: The past of the present in Zambia.* Lund University.

Kamwanga, J., Macwan'gi, M., & Geest, J. (1999). *Health reforms and the quality of health care in Zambia.* Spinhuis Publishers.

Kelly, M. J. (1999). *The origins and developments of education in Zambia from Pre-Colonial Time to 1996: A book of notes and readings.* Image Publishers.

Klasen, S. (2002). Low schooling for girls, slower growth for all? Cross-country evidence on the effect of gender inequality in education on economic development. *The World Bank Economic Review, 16*(3), 345–373.

Lloyd, C. B., Kaufman, C. E., & Hewett, P. (2000). The spread of primary schooling in sub-Saharan Africa: Implications for fertility change. *Population and Development Review, 26*(3), 483–515.

Martin, A. (1972). *Minding their own Business: Zambia's struggle against western control.*

Masaiti, G., & Chita, J. (2014). Zambia: An overview of formal education. *Education in East Central Africa, 16*, 423.

Masiye, F., Chitah, B. M., Chanda, P., & Simeo, F. (2008). Removal of user fees at primary health care facilities in Zambia: A study of the effects on utilisation and quality of care. *Regional Network for Equity in Health in East and Southern Africa Discussion Paper, 57*.

Nakazwe, C., Michelo, C., Sandøy, I. F., & Fylkesnes, K. (2019). Contrasting HIV prevalence trends among young women and men in Zambia in the past 12 years: Data from demographic and health surveys 2002–2014. *BMC Infectious Diseases, 19*(1), 432.

Nkosha, D. C., & Mwanza, P. (2009). Quality of basic education provided by rural community and regular schools in the Northern province of Zambia. *Journal of International Cooperation in Education, 12*(1), 19–32.

Shaw, T. M. (1982). Zambia after twenty years: Recession and repression without revolution. *African Issues, 12*(1–2), 53–58.

UNESCO. (2015). *Education for all global monitoring report regional overview: Sub-Saharan Africa*. UNESCO Paris.

Whitworth, A. (2015). Explaining Zambian poverty: A history of (nonagriculture) economic policy since independence. *Journal of International Development, 27*(7), 953–986.

World Bank. (2017). *Educating girls, ending child marriage*.

World Bank. (2019). *Population growth in Zambia*. Retrieved from: https://data.worldbank.org/indicator/SP.POP.TOTL?locations=ZM.

4

Theory and Previous Research

Abstract This chapter delves into theories explaining Africa's postcolonial economic development, with a focus on institutions, human capital, and the often-overlooked role of Christian missionaries. It explores how initial colonial setups, particularly missionary activities in education and healthcare, have lasting impacts on contemporary development. Through a concise examination of existing research, the chapter sets the stage for understanding the nuanced dynamics shaping Africa's post-independence economic trajectory.

Keywords Long-term development • Christian missionaries • Health • Education • Sub-Saharan Africa • Zambia

Growth economists who have sought to understand why economic development has lagged in Africa in comparison to other regions of the world have theorized that Africa's poverty trap has been a result of the form of European colonialism that characterized a region (Acemoglu et al., 2001, 2002). The underlying assumption behind this theory is that, in regions where European settlers settled in numbers (settler colonies), they

M. Chanda Chiseni, *The Economic Impact of Christian Missionaries in Zambia*,
https://doi.org/10.1007/978-3-031-65304-9_4

introduced development-oriented institutions that typified their places of origin, such as strong private property rights. In contrast, in regions where Europeans did not settle in large numbers (non-settler colonies), they implemented "extractive" institutions that sequestered local populations from participating in political or economic affairs (Robinson & Acemoglu, 2012). The theory that a region's colonial legacy determines its postcolonial development trajectory is predicated on the premise that institutions are important for development.

The notion that institutions are imperative for economic development has been championed by North (1991). North (1991) defines institutions as "humanely devised constraints that structure political, economic and social interactions." He further asserts that given a set of constraints (institutions) in the real world, individuals select combination choices that award the most economic benefits. This process is intended to lead people to an ideal economic position. In their earlier assertions, North and Thomas (1973) vehemently argued that the set of institutions adopted by society are key in determining economic development both cross-sectionally and across time. Furthermore, they proposed that the inability of Third World countries to adopt institutions that protect property rights has been a key source of economic underdevelopment.

The extant literature contends that contemporary institutional variations are key in explaining the diverging economic trajectories in developing regions (Acemoglu et al., 2001, 2002; La Porta et al., 1997, 1998). Therefore, this literature has focused its attention on understanding the origins of the institutional variations. This literature proposes that the postcolonial institutional variations in developing countries can be traced back to their colonizers. Consequently, it is these institutional variations that have produced divergent growth paths. Acemoglu et al. (2001) look at the impact of colonial institutions on economic development. La Porta et al. (1997, 1998) seek to understand the impact of legal origins on long-run development. Other studies have explored the impact of legal origins on military conscription (Mulligan & Shleifer, 2005), the regulation of labour markets (Botero et al., 2004), the enforcement of contracts (Djankov et al., 2003) and (Acemoglu & Johnson, 2005), the comparative advantage of a country (Nunn, 2007), a country's economic growth trajectory (Mahoney, 2001) and female HIV infection rate (Anderson,

2018). Bernhard et al. (2004) analyze the long-term effects of colonialism on the democratic survival of postcolonial democracies; survival and length of colonial rule only hold for the former British colonies.

Most of the literature that has contributed to the colonial legacies debate had initially focused its attention on studying diverging postcolonial economic development based on the broad identity of the colonial power (Acemoglu et al., 2001; Bernhard et al., 2004; Botero et al., 2004; La Porta et al., 2008; Nunn, 2007). Within the broader colonial structures, it is only recently that other political, religious, and economic actors have begun receiving attention regarding their role in shaping postcolonial developmental outcomes (Lankina & Getachew, 2021). Within the generic colonial power identities, the actors that have lately received more attention are the Christian missionaries. In most colonial territories, missionaries were important actors in that they provided the lion's share of two key elements of human capital development education (Baten et al., 2021; Bolt & Bezemer, 2009; Fourie & Swanepoel, 2015; Frankema, 2012; Gallego & Woodberry, 2010; Montgomery, 2017; Nunn, 2010; Nunn et al., 2014) and health (Doyle et al., 2019; Gallego & Woodberry, 2010; Hardiman, 2006; Walima T Kalusa, 2014). For this reason, in the next section, I consider how historical human capital investments by missionaries may affect long-run development.

Human Capital Investment and Long-Run Development

The concept of human capital was coined by Schultz (1961); he asserted that knowledge and skill are a type of capital, and deliberate investment in human capital may spur economic output and individual earnings. More broadly, Ehrlich and Murphy (2007) define human capital as "an intangible asset, best thought of as a stock of embodied and disembodied knowledge, comprising education, information, health, entrepreneurship, and productive and innovative skills, which is formed through investments in schooling, job training, and health, as well as through research and development projects and informal knowledge transfers."

Schultz (1961) postulated that the puzzles that characterize dynamic and growing economies could be solved once human investment is accounted for. He observed that farmworkers who took on non-farm jobs earned significantly less than industrial workers of similar age, sex, and race. These differences in earnings can be explained by differences in education and health (Schultz, 1961). This book focuses on understanding the colonial investments in public education and health and how these affect long-run human development.

The recent literature has used colonial institutional variations to explain differences in post-colonial development trajectories (Acemoglu et al., 2001, 2002; La Porta et al., 1997, 1998). Offering an alternative view, Lipset (1960) suggests that causation runs from human capital development and growth in income to institutional development. Bolt and Bezemer (2009) postulate that institutional differences may not entirely explain the differential paths in post-colonial development in Africa, but rather by the fact that colonial settlers brought with them their human capital and the necessary resources required to increase the education aspect of human capital via the provision of formal education. The colonial settlers also initiated Western-styled healthcare in Africa (Jennings, 2019; Vaughan, 1994); they essentially brought the necessary human capital and resources to establish and expand Western-healthcare.

Since the white settlers brought and developed human capital through the provision of formal education, the initial endowment of human capital in the various colonies is expected to have a long-term impact on development. Exploiting this notion, Krueger and Lindahl (2001) find a positive correlation between the initial level of education and economic growth. Lipset (1960) also shows that individuals with a higher level of education are more cognizant of their government actions, better able to participate in the affairs of society, and likely to settle differences through the ballot and negotiations rather than through violent clashes. In effect, human capital growth leads to efficient policies and political stability. Reinforcing this view, Glaeser et al. (2004) provide empirical evidence showing that human capital development positively impacts political institutions and leads to economic growth. Castelló-Climent (2008) shows that mass education impacts democracy through the implementation and sustainability of democracies.

Bush and Saltarelli (2000) posited that education might be used as a tool for cultural repression and ethnic division. For example, during the colonial period, more especially in Belgian Africa, minority groups that received an education ruled over the majority, as in the case of Burundi and Rwanda, where the Tutsi minority were favored over the Hutu majority, hence received access to better schooling. Ethnic favoritism by the colonial government ultimately culminated in the 1990s genocide. Badru (2010) cites another example where colonial ethnic favoritism led to violent clashes. In Liberia, the colonial government favored Americo-Liberians who received first-class citizen benefits, such as quality education, hence, more economic opportunities than the Africans. The segregation of the Africans ultimately led to chaos where "the rule of the gun undermined the rule of law." The examples cited above show that elite education compared to broad-based education may have long-run negative effects. The empirical evidence presented by Dias and Tebaldi (2012) also shows that human capital investments affect long-run economic growth. Still, it takes some time for the accumulation of human capital to translate into growth.

Health is also an important aspect of human capital formation and can contribute to economic growth in several ways. Good health among the labour-force increases productivity and lowers work absenteeism, which raises production (Petchko, 2018). Kalemli-Ozcan et al. (2000) indicate that improvements in health increase the incentives to obtain more education because investment in education can be repaid over a longer working life span. Well (2007) avers that a healthier school-going population is correlated with lower absenteeism and higher cognitive functioning, which raises schooling performance. The idea is that access to good health bolsters the process of knowledge acquisition, increases schooling, and improves the quality of human capital over time, thus fostering economic growth (Petchko, 2018). The study by Huillery (2009) shows that, for French West Africa, 30 percent of contemporary economic performance can be explained by colonial investments in public goods such as education, health, and infrastructure. In effect, she demonstrates that colonial health investments significantly determine current health performance, colonial investments in education affect current educational performance, and current infrastructure development is determined by colonial infrastructure development. The study also finds that regions with more colonial investments continued to have a higher concentration because of the persistent nature of physical facilities and positive spillovers on local demand for these investments. Ricart-Huguet (2022) compares how colonial public education and health investments affected long-run development in British and French Africa. In this study, he finds that non-extractive colonial investments such as education and health explain current economic development, access to healthcare, and educational attainment in French and British Africa, especially in French Africa.

Christian missionaries were important colonial actors that contributed to the human capital accumulation in Northern Rhodesia via the provision of broad-based education and healthcare (Calvi & Mantovanelli, 2018; Chiseni & Bolt, 2022; Jennings, 2019; Vaughan, 1994). Considering the missionary legacy of human capital development in Africa, the extant literature has endeavored to understand the impact of missionary exposure on long-run development. Lankina and Getachew (2021) and Woodberry (2004) find a positive correlation between the historical presence of missionaries and democracy. Nunn (2009) finds evidence showing that, through increased education, Protestant missionaries proliferate the incidence of attitudes that favour democracy and civic participation. Fourie and Swanepoel (2015) show that Africans who lived in districts with missionaries in 1849 exhibited higher levels of education 150 years later. Alesina et al. (2021) find that main mission stations in Africa are significantly related to current intergenerational mobility and educational attainment. In Benin, Wantchekon et al. (2015) document positive human capital externalities from religious schools. The study finds a positive treatment effect of education on living standards for first-generation students and their descendants; additionally, it finds that they are more likely to have a political voice and less likely to be farmers. Meier zu Selhausen (2014) links missionary exposure in Uganda to female empowerment. Meier Zu Selhausen (2019) examines the origins and long-term development of African mass education in colonial Sub-Saharan Africa. The study accentuates the importance of African agency, local demand, and the supply of missionary-trained African teachers in the development of mass education. For other regions,

Valencia Caicedo (2019) shows a positive effect of missionaries on educational attainment in South America; Mantovanelli (2014) and Castelló-Climent et al. (2015) show that missionaries had a positive impact on literacy and tertiary education in India.

A critical assessment of the literature on the long-run impacts of human capital investment reveals the following mechanisms through which Christian missionary investment in education and health may affect development today. The missionaries used their educational and health platforms to teach the fundamental Christian ethos to those that received their services. Hardiman (2006) pointed out that while patients were waiting to receive treatment at the missionary hospitals, the missionaries used this opportunity to preach the gospel. Additionally, Kelly (1999) also indicated that the purpose of missionary education was to equip Africans to participate in the colonial economy and enable the converts to read the bible, more so for the Protestant than Catholic missionaries.

In essence, missionaries were agents of human capital formation and agents of cultural transformation. Bisin and Verdier (2000) have argued that preferences, values, and social norms are formed and transmitted across generations over time via various cultural interactive processes. The following studies also establish from an empirical standpoint the enduring impacts of culture on various contemporary outcomes, economic development in Europe (Guiso et al., 2003; Tabellini, 2010), and violence in the USA and Germany (Grosjean, 2014; Voigtländer & Voth, 2012). It is possible then that exposure to Christian missionaries over a long period may shape societal norms and values which persist over time (Mantovanelli, 2013). The link between religion and long-term economic growth was formalized by Weber (1905), who pointed out that Protestant ethics such as hard work, wealth creation, and literacy fostered economic prosperity, inculcated a capitalist spirit and led societies on a path of industrialization. Nunn (2014) also postulates that culture may shape institutions that promote long-term economic growth.

Moreover, through the provision of broad education, missionaries increased the accessibility to formal education for the local population, raising the level of the educated population. Bolt and Bezemer (2009) pointed out that an increase in the level of the educated colonial African population altered current levels of education and fostered long-term economic growth. Bisin and Verdier (2000) indicated that values and social norms are transmissible across generations; therefore, the missionaries could have instilled the value for formal education in the indigenous people, which ultimately transmitted to generations that followed; henceforth increasing the current levels of education. Moreover, Huillery (2009) also indicated that colonial education infrastructure positively determines current schooling infrastructure; in essence, current educational levels could have been affected by the persistence in schooling infrastructure largely established by missionaries.

Additionally, missionaries emphasized that those who converted to Christianity must embrace the Christian values and ways of living; for example, the missionaries taught abstinence from sex until marriage monogamy, and they taught against contraceptives. Through the generational transmission of values and social norms (Bisin & Verdier, 2000), it is therefore expected that those exposed to missionary praxis pass on these doctrines to subsequent generations.

Lowes and Montero (2021) find that African colonial medical experiences in Central Africa shape contemporary attitudes towards medicine. More precisely, the study indicates that greater exposure to forced colonial medical campaigns reduces current trust in medicine; additionally, the study finds that World Bank projects in the health sector are less successful in areas with greater exposure to colonial medical campaigns. Huillery (2009) also indicates that colonial investments in healthcare infrastructure positively determined current healthcare infrastructure. More recently, Baumert (2022) found that in Cameroon, regions exposed to institutionalized medical facilities during the late interwar period exhibit a higher density of public hospitals and non-hospital medical facilities today. He asserts that this may be driven by the acceptance of Western healthcare, a strong political voice and human capital accumulation of the Africans. Because of the persistence of colonial missionary healthcare infrastructure, it is possible that individuals who live in regions that received more missionary healthcare may still have access to these facilities. As indicated by Kalemli-Ozcan et al. (2000) and Petchko (2018), access to healthcare increases the incentives to obtain more education and increase worker productivity hence fostering long-run economic growth. Well (2007) shows that access to healthcare lowers absenteeism and increases cognitive function; hence, access to good health may increase educational attainment.

References

Acemoglu, D., & Johnson, S. (2005). Unbundling institutions. *Journal of Political Economy, 113*(5), 949–995.

Acemoglu, D., Johnson, S., & Robinson, J. A. (2001). The colonial origins of comparative development: An empirical investigation. *American Economic Review, 91*(5), 1369–1401.

Acemoglu, D., Johnson, S., & Robinson, J. A. (2002). Reversal of fortune: Geography and Institutions in the making of the Modern World Income Distribution. *The Quarterly Journal of Economics, 117*(4), 1231–1294.

Alesina, A., Hohmann, S., Michalopoulos, S., & Papaioannou, E. (2021). Intergenerational mobility in Africa. *Econometrica, 89*(1), 1–35.

Anderson, S. (2018). Legal origins and female HIV. *American Economic Review, 108*(6), 1407–1439.

Badru, P. (2010). Ethnic conflict and state formation in post-colonial Africa: A comparative study of ethnic genocide in the Congo, Liberia, Nigeria, and Rwanda-Burundi. *Journal of Third World Studies, 27*(2), 149–169.

Baten, J., de Haas, M., Kempter, E., & zu Selhausen, F. M. (2021). Educational gender inequality in Sub-Saharan Africa: A long-term perspective. *Population and Development Review, 47*, 813–849.

Baumert, N. (2022). *On a mission for public health: The Historical roots of Institutionalized health care in colonial Cameroon*. Lund University.

Bernhard, M., Reenock, C., & Nordstrom, T. (2004). The legacy of Western overseas colonialism on democratic survival. *International Studies Quarterly, 48*(1), 225–250.

Bisin, A., & Verdier, T. (2000). "Beyond the melting pot": Cultural transmission, marriage, and the evolution of ethnic and religious traits. *The Quarterly Journal of Economics, 115*(3), 955–988.

Bolt, J., & Bezemer, D. (2009). Understanding long-run African growth: Colonial Institutions or Colonial Education? *The Journal of Development Studies, 45*(1), 24–54.

Botero, J. C., Djankov, S., Porta, R. L., Lopez-de-Silanes, F., & Shleifer, A. (2004). The regulation of labour. *The Quarterly Journal of Economics, 119*(4), 1339–1382.
Bush, K. D., & Saltarelli, D. (2000). *The two faces of education in ethnic conflict: Towards a peacebuilding education for children*. University of York.
Calvi, R., & Mantovanelli, F. G. (2018). Long-term effects of access to health care: Medical missions in colonial India. *Journal of Development Economics, 135*, 285–303.
Castelló-Climent, A. (2008). On the distribution of education and democracy. *Journal of Development Economics, 87*(2), 179–190.
Castelló-Climent, A., Chaudhary, L., & Mukhopadhyay, A. (2015). *Tertiary Education and Prosperity: Catholic missionaries to luminosity in India*.
Chiseni, M. C., & Bolt, J. (2022). Left behind: Tracing the roots of regional and gender inequality in education in Zambia 1924–1990. Unpublished research paper.
Dias, J., & Tebaldi, E. (2012). Institutions, human capital, and growth: The institutional mechanism. *Structural Change and Economic Dynamics, 23*(3), 300–312.
Djankov, S., La Porta, R., Lopez-de-Silanes, F., & Shleifer, A. (2003). Courts. *The Quarterly Journal of Economics, 118*(2), 453–517.
Doyle, S., Meier zu Selhausen, F., & Weisdorf, J. (2019). The blessings of medicine? Patient characteristics and health outcomes in a Ugandan Mission Hospital, 1908–19701. *Social History of Medicine*. https://doi.org/10.1093/shm/hky125
Ehrlich, I., & Murphy, K. M. (2007). Why does human capital need a journal? *Journal of Human Capital, 1*(1), 1–7.
Fourie, J., & Swanepoel, C. (2015). *When selection trumps persistence: The lasting effect of missionary education in South Africa*. International Institute of Social History.
Frankema, E. H. (2012). The origins Africa: Was British rule more benign? *European Review of Economic History, 16*(4), 335–355.
Gallego, F. A., & Woodberry, R. (2010). Christian missionaries and education in former African colonies: How competition mattered. *Journal of African Economies, 19*(3), 294–329.
Glaeser, E. L., La Porta, R., Lopez-de-Silanes, F., & Shleifer, A. (2004). Do institutions cause growth? *Journal of Economic Growth, 9*(3), 271–303.
Grosjean, P. (2014). A history of violence: The culture of honor and homicide in the US South. *Journal of the European Economic Association, 12*(5), 1285–1316.

Guiso, L., Sapienza, P., & Zingales, L. (2003). People's opium? Religion and economic attitudes. *Journal of Monetary Economics, 50*(1), 225–282.
Hardiman, D. (2006). Healing bodies, saving souls: medical missions in Asia and Africa (Vol. 80): Rodopi.
Huillery, E. (2009). History matters: The long-term impact of colonial public investments in French West Africa. *American Economic Journal: Applied Economics, 1*(2), 176–215.
Jennings, M. (2019). Cooperation and competition: Missions, the colonial state and constructing a health system in colonial Tanganyika. In *Beyond the state* (pp. 153–173). Manchester University Press.
Kalemli-Ozcan, S., Ryder, H. E., & Weil, D. N. (2000). Mortality decline, human capital investment, and economic growth. *Journal of Development Economics, 62*(1), 1–23.
Kalusa, W. T. (2014). Missionaries, African patients, and negotiating missionary medicine at Kalene Hospital, Zambia, 1906–1935. *Journal of Southern African Studies, 40*(2), 283–294.
Kelly, M. J. (1999). *The origins and Developments of Education in Zambia from Pre-Colonial Time to 1996*: A Book of Notes and Readings: Image Publishers.
Krueger, A. B., & Lindahl, M. (2001). Education for growth: Why and for whom? *Journal of Economic Literature, 39*(4), 1101–1136.
La Porta, R., Lopez-de-Silanes, F., & Shleifer, A. (2008). The economic consequences of legal origins. *Journal of Economic Literature, 46*(2), 285–332.
La Porta, R., Lopez-de-Silanes, F., Shleifer, A., & Vishny, R. W. (1997). Legal determinants of external finance. *The Journal of Finance, 52*(3), 1131–1150.
La Porta, R., Lopez-de-Silanes, F., Shleifer, A., & Vishny, R. W. (1998). Law and finance. *Journal of Political Economy, 106*(6), 1113–1155.
Lankina, T., & Getachew, L. (2021). Mission or empire, word or sword? The human capital legacy in postcolonial democratic development. In *Critical readings in the history of Christian Mission* (pp. 887–921). Brill.
Lipset, S. M. (1960). *Political man. The social bases of politics garden city*. Doubleday.
Lowes, S., & Montero, E. (2021). The legacy of colonial medicine in Central Africa. *American Economic Review, 111*(4), 1284–1314.
Mahoney, P. G. (2001). The common law and economic growth: Hayek might be right. *The Journal of Legal Studies, 30*(2), 503–525.
Mantovanelli, F. (2013). *Christian missions, HIV and sexual behaviour in Sub-Saharan Africa*. Available at SSRN 2413178.
Mantovanelli, F. (2014). *The Protestant legacy: Missions and literacy in India*. Available at SSRN 2413170.

Meier zu Selhausen, F. (2014). Missionaries and female empowerment in colonial Uganda: New evidence from Protestant marriage registers, 1880–1945. *Economic History of Developing Regions, 29*(1), 74–112.
Meier zu Selhausen, F. (2019). Missions, education and conversion in Colonial Africa. In D. Mitch & G. Cappelli (Eds.), *Globalization and the rise of mass education* (Palgrave Studies in Economic History) (pp. 25–59). Palgrave Macmillan.
Montgomery, M. (2017). Colonial legacy of gender inequality: Christian missionaries in German East Africa. *Politics Society, 45*(2), 225–268.
Mulligan, C. B., & Shleifer, A. (2005). Conscription as regulation. *American Law and Economics Review, 7*(1), 85–111.
North, D. C. (1991). *Institutions. Journal of economic perspectives, 5*(1), 97–112.
North, D. C., & Thomas, R. P. (1973). *The rise of the western world: A new economic history*. Cambridge University Press.
Nunn, N. (2007). Relationship-specificity, incomplete contracts, and the pattern of trade. *The Quarterly Journal of Economics, 122*(2), 569–600.
Nunn, N. (2009). *Christians in colonial Africa*. Unpublished manuscript.
Nunn, N. (2010). Religious conversion in colonial Africa. *American Economic Review, 100*(2), 147–152.
Nunn, N., Akyeampong, E., Bates, R., & Robinson, J. A. (2014). Gender and missionary influence in colonial Africa. In *African development in historical perspective*. Harvard University.
Petchko, K. (2018). *How to write about economics and public policy*. Academic Press.
Ricart-Huguet, J. (2022). Why colonial investments persist more in Francophone than Anglophone Africa. *Journal of Historical Political Economy, 1*(2), 477–498.
Robinson, J. A., & Acemoglu, D. (2012). *Why nations fail: The origins of power, prosperity and poverty*. Profile London.
Schultz, T. W. (1961). Investment in human capital. *The American Economic Review, 51*(1), 1–17.
Tabellini, G. (2010). Culture and institutions: economic development in the regions of Europe. *Journal of the European Economic Association, 8*(4), 677–716.
Valencia Caicedo, F. (2019). The mission: Human capital transmission, economic persistence, and culture in South America. *The Quarterly Journal of Economics, 134*(1), 507–556.
Vaughan, M. (1994). Health and hegemony: Representation of disease and the creation of the colonial subject in Nyasaland. In *Contesting colonial hegemony: State and society in Africa and India* (pp. 173–201). I B Tauris.

Voigtländer, N., & Voth, H.-J. (2012). Persecution perpetuated: The medieval origins of anti-Semitic violence in Nazi Germany. *The Quarterly Journal of Economics, 127*(3), 1339–1392.
Wantchekon, L., Klašnja, M., & Novta, N. (2015). Education and human capital externalities: Evidence from colonial Benin. *The Quarterly Journal of Economics, 130*(2), 703–757.
Weber, M. (1905). The Protestant ethic and the spirit of capitalism. *Trans. Talcott Parsons.*
Well, D. N. (2007). Accounting for the effect of health on economic growth. *The Quarterly Journal of Economics, 122*(3), 1265–1306.
Woodberry, R. D. (2004). *The shadow of empire: Christian missions, colonial policy, and democracy in postcolonial societies.* University of North Carolina at Chapel Hill Manuscript.

5

Methodology

Abstract In this chapter, I outline the data sources and empirical approaches employed to explore the enduring economic effects of Christian missionaries in Zambia. Utilizing a diverse range of historical, geographical, and contemporary data, I employ distinct empirical strategies. Furthermore, I address the inherent limitations of the data.

Keywords Long-term development • Christian missionaries • Health • Education • Sub-Saharan Africa • Zambia

Data

Colonial Data Sources

In this study, I draw quantitative data from various historical sources. From 1890 to 1924, Northern Rhodesia was under the administration of the British South African Company (BSAC). As pointed out by Gann (1969) and Gelfand (1961), under the rulership of BSAC, data collection in the territory was sparse; the Company did not invest resources to

M. Chanda Chiseni, *The Economic Impact of Christian Missionaries in Zambia*,
https://doi.org/10.1007/978-3-031-65304-9_5

bolster its capacity to collect data, especially for the African population. When the British colonial government took over the administration of Northern Rhodesia from the Company, they formally established various departments responsible for providing various public services and collecting data. The departments of African education and health were formalized under the rulership of the British colonial government. Though data collection was not always consistent, data collection under the British colonial government was more pronounced than when the Company administrated Northern Rhodesia.

Missionary Stations

Most studies that have analyzed the persistent effects of missionaries in Africa have utilized missionary station location data from the following missionary atlases: Dennis et al. (1903), Béthune (1889), and (Roome, 1925). As argued by Jedwab et al. (2022), these sources underreport the locations of missionary stations. Additionally, missionary stations were not static but increased incrementally over the colonial period. Figure 5.1 compares the missionary locations reported in the world missionary atlases and the missionaries I digitized from the ecclesiastical reports from 1924 to 1948. From Fig. 5.1, it can be seen that nineteen Catholic and Protestant missionary stations are reported by atlases Dennis et al. (1903), Béthune (1889), and 63 Protestant and Catholic missionary stations reported by Roome (1925). There are 212 Protestant and Catholic missionary stations that are reported in the Northern Rhodesian Ecclesiastical reports; there are fundamentally 91 percent missionary stations omitted in Dennis et al. (1903), Béthune (1889), and 71 percent missionary stations omitted in Roome (1925). Most of the world missionary atlases capture missionaries at a single point in time; this study uses detailed information on missionary locations that I collected from the Colonial blue books' ecclesiastical records. I geocode Protestant and Catholic missionary stations in Northern Rhodesia from 1924 to 1948.

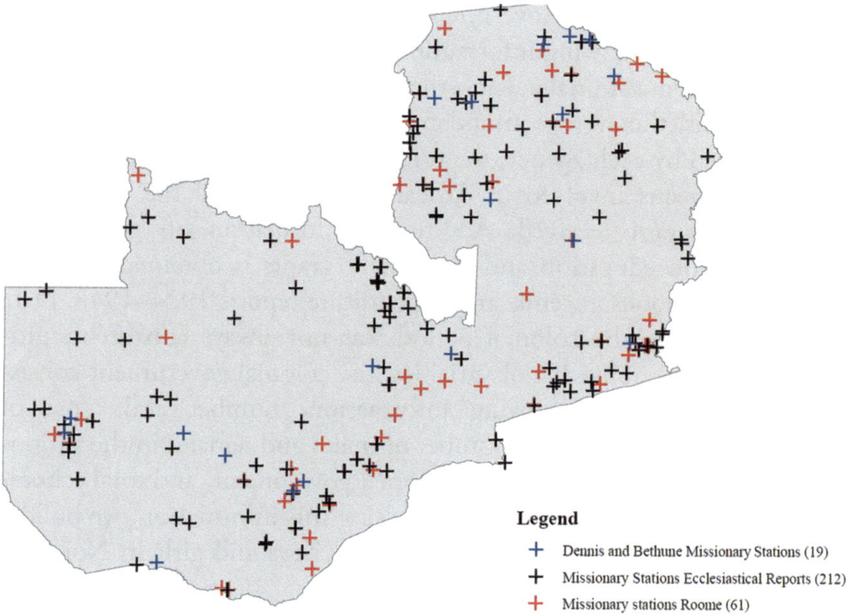

Fig. 5.1 Comparing missionary stations from world missionary atlases and Northern Rhodesian Ecclesiastical reports. (Source: Drawn by Author)

Education

During the Company's rule, the provision of education by the various missionary agencies was independent of the British South African Company; hence, missionary societies did not receive any financial aid from the BSAC for their education provision mission (Snelson, 1974). After taking over the administration of Northern Rhodesia from BSAC, the British colonial office established a sub-department of African education. The missionary societies that sought funding from the colonial government to provide education had to adhere to a strict native education code defined in the Native Educational Ordinance of 1937 (Kelly, 1999). The information on the various agencies that received aid from the government was published in the returns to Native education reports. In the African education reports, I identify four different education agents in the data: Protestant missionaries, Catholic missionaries,

Native Authorities, and Government. The African school returns report also provide the following information, the number of schools administered by each educational agency, the number of boys and girls enrolled in the schools, the average attendance, school fees, voluntary contributions received by each agency, the total expenditure on education, number of Europeans involved in African education, and the amount of government grant received. Additional information on government expenditure on education and missionary grants is obtained from the Colonial blue books' revenue and expenditure reports 1924–1948. Data collection during the colonial period was not always consistent; ultimately, from the above list of variables, the colonial government consistently recorded the following information, number and types of educational agents, the total number of males and females in the various schools, grants received from the colonial government, and total schooling expenditure per schooling agent. Using this information, we build a panel data capturing educational access for boys and girls in Northern Rhodesia from 1925 to 1953 (20 years).

Healthcare

The British colonial government had established the colonial medical department to provide healthcare in the territory. The colonial medical department kept records of the medical work conducted in the territory in the colonial medical reports. Though these reports contain a plethora of information, the information was not consistently recorded during the colonial period. For example, the work of the medical missionaries is only reported in the medical reports from 1933, while the government's medical work is reported from 1924. The medical reports provide information on the number of outpatients and inpatients treated at colonial African and missionary hospitals. The medical reports also provide detailed information on the various diseases diagnosed upon admission in African colonial hospitals and the number of people who died yearly. However, the number of deaths recorded were not consistent throughout the colonial period.

Additionally, the colonial medical records contain information on the location of colonial government and missionary hospitals in Northern Rhodesia. For much of the colonial period, the British government operated about 12 African hospitals, and by 1953, the Protestant and Catholic missionaries had established 89 hospitals in Northern Rhodesia. I geocode the exact locations of the African colonial hospitals and missionary hospitals from 1925 to 1953.

Historical Geographical Data

When penetrating the inland, the missionaries followed the explorer routes that previous European explorers mapped. Figure 5.2 illustrates the various European explorers that explored Northern Rhodesia; one of

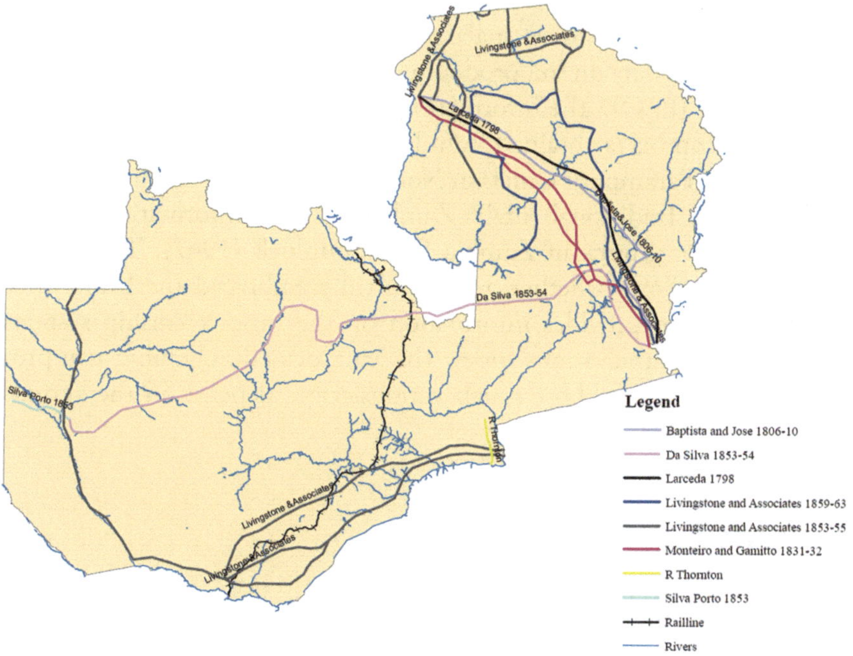

Fig. 5.2 Missionary explorer routes in Northern Rhodesia. (Source: Drawn by Author)

the most prominent and renowned explorers in Northern Rhodesia was David Livingstone; he is believed to have opened up Northern Rhodesia to many Protestant missionaries. I draw information on historical missionary explorer routes from Davies (1971) and Nunn and Wantchekon (2011). I digitize the historical railway line in Northern Rhodesia using contemporary data developed by DIVA-GIS. I also digitize historical rivers in Zambia using information from OKI.

Furthermore, I digitize the location of historical mines using the information I collected from Juif and Frankema (2018). I use the information on historical population densities and cities from Klein Goldewijk et al. (2010). Moreover, Klein Goldewijk et al. (2010) provide information on the grazing land size available in the various African countries and how much of the land is rainfed and the cropland size. The data on the African coastline is obtained from the African Marine Atlas (AMA). I acquired Zambia's geographical boundary data from the New York University (NYU) spatial repository.

This study uses historical malaria ecology data from Kiszewski et al. (2004). I obtain data on soil productivity from the Food and Agricultural Organization (FAO). The information on the various maize plantations in colonial Zambia is obtained from Jenkin (2018). I collect information on the ruling Paramount Chiefs in Northern Rhodesia from the Ministry of Chiefs and Traditional Affairs Zambia. I obtain information on precolonial ethnic groups in Zambia from Murdock (1967). This ethnographic atlas shows whether a specific tribe embraced the bride price tradition. It also provides information on the various kinship systems practiced within the various tribes. The Murdock ethnographic atlas provides information on how much various tribes depend on the various agriculture modes.

Current Data

To study the long-term effects of missionaries, I use various micro cross-sectional contemporary data sets. To analyze the enduring effects of missionaries on education, I use the 1990 Zambian individual-level Census Population, Housing and Agriculture data provided by IPUMS. The census provides information on various individual and household characteristics. Crucial for this study's empirical strategy is the birthplace of the individual. This variable allows me to determine the Euclidean distance from an individual's birthplace to a missionary station; the study uses proximity to a mission station as a proxy for missionary exposure. To determine the long-term impact of missionary praxis on HIV and related sexual behavior, this study uses three waves of the Zambian Demographic Health Survey, specifically, the 2007, 2014, and 2018–2019 surveys. The Zambian DHS data is a nationally represented sample containing information on individuals from 13,625 households. The DHS data sets employed in this analysis contain biomarkers for sexually transmitted diseases; these are biological measures of an individual's health condition. The individual's HIV status information is not self-reported data but actual HIV test results. Upon surveying individuals, the DHS agents[1] collect dried blood samples (DBSs), which are then sent to the laboratory for HIV testing. As of 2007, the DHS provided georeferenced data for various household groupings, referred to as clusters. To ensure respondent confidentiality, GPS coordinates for urban clusters have 2 kilometers of error, and rural clusters have 5 kilometers of positional error. The georeferenced data is crucial for my empirical strategy; it allows me to measure the distance from a respondent's place of residence to the closest missionary station and hospitals. I use these distances as proxies for missionary exposure. Additionally, I use a data set on current hospitals in Sub-Saharan Africa locations provided by Maina et al. (2019).

Methods

Missionary Expansion

To capture the synchronic and diachronic impact of missionaries over space and time, I amalgamate various first-hand historical data sources and contemporary data sources and analyze the impact of missionary exposure within a quantitative framework.

[1] More information on biomarkers can be found here https://dhsprogram.com/

As a first step, I explore the determinants of the patterns of missionary settlement in Northern Rhodesia from 1924 to 1953. Fundamentally, the impetus of this analysis is to understand why missionaries were choosing certain locations to build mission stations and churches over others. This analysis is paramount for subsequent long-run estimations in this study because, to closely capture the long-term impact of Christian missionaries in Africa, it is pertinent to understand the drivers of missionary expansion in Africa. If the determinants of missionary expansion are not understood and not controlled for when estimating the long-term impact of Christian missionary exposure, the estimation results may be laden with endogenous bias.

To ascertain the determinants of Missionary expansion in Northern Rhodesia from 1924 to 1953, I partition Zambia into 7134 grid cells of the size 11.1 × 11.1 km. With these partitions, I determine the historical-geographical features of each cell. Using ArcMap, I calculate the average historical population density within each cell, the mean grazing land size, rainfed land size, soil productivity, land elevation, and ruggedness. I determine whether there is a mission station, city, maize plant, and Paramount Chief within each cell.

In addition, I measure Euclidean distances from the centroid of each cell to the nearest river, railway line, mine, and coast explorer route. I repeat this process for every year from 1924 to 1948. Ultimately, I build a novel data set that captures missionary stations expansion between 1924 and 1948 (24 years), containing 176,925 observations. I repeat the procedure outlined above to determine the factors that influenced missionary hospital expansion in Northern Rhodesia. Additionally, I determine whether there is a missionary hospital within each grid cell from 1933 to 1953 (20 years). Consequently, after determining the annual characteristics of each grid cell, I construct a balanced panel data set with 135,546 observations.

One panel data encapsulates the expansion of mission stations from 1925 to 1948, and the other the expansion of hospitals from 1933 to 1953. In the first step, I analyze the factors that determined the expansion of missionary stations in Northern Rhodesia. To this aim, I construct a dichotomous variable that captures whether a mission station was present within a given grid cell annually from 1925 to 1948. I then use this dichotomous variable as an outcome variable to calculate the probability of a mission station being present within a specific cell, given the various cell characteristics. In the second step, I ascertain the determinants of missionary hospital expansion by first constructing a dichotomous variable that determines whether a missionary hospital was present within a given cell annually from 1933 to 1953. Using this dichotomous variable as my main outcome variable, I calculate the likelihood of establishing a mission hospital in a specific cell region given the cell characteristics. For all the estimations, I included year fixed effects. This paper estimates all the models using an Ordinal Generalized Linear Model (OGLM) with a probit link.

Christian Missionaries and Education

To ascertain the impact of missionary exposure on education, I first build panel data that captures the development and accessibility of formal education in Northern Rhodesia from 1925 to 1954. The panel data captures the total number of schools that the various educational agents operated, the total number of boys and girls that were enrolled in their schools, the amount they spent on education, for the Protestant and Catholic agents' information on the number of grants that were annually received from the government is available.

In the second step, I amalgamate the individual level 1990 census data with the historical, geographical data and missionary station location data. In ArcMap, I draw 30 km buffers around each place of birth. The buffers allow the study to calculate average values of selected historical-geographical features. Within each 30 kms buffer around the place of birth, I measure the average land elevation. Additionally, I measure Euclidean distances from the individual's place of birth to the nearest mission station, railway line, river, explorer route, coastline, and mine.

Within an Ordinary Least Squares framework, the study determines the extent of the gender gap between Protestant and Catholic schools. Consequently, I use the Euclidean distance from the individual's place of birth to the nearest mission station as a proxy for missionary exposure. Using this proxy, I estimate the effect of nearness to a mission station on educational attainment for individuals born in the precolonial and postcolonial periods. In the latter regression, I control for various selected factors that may have influenced missionary expansion; I control for these factors to ameliorate endogenous bias in our model. Additionally, the novelty of the individual-level data allows the study to control for tribal, provincial, and birth cohort fixed effects.

Christian Missionaries and Health

To study the effects of Christian missionaries on health, I firstly use descriptive statistics to analyze the extent of missionary and secular medical outreach in Northern Rhodesia and gauge the trained Africans' level of participation in the colonial health sector. To measure the extent of outreach between missionaries and the colonial government, I compare the number of missionary hospitals and African colonial hospitals established in Northern Rhodesia from 1925 to 1953. Furthermore, I determine how frequently African outpatients attended missionary hospitals relative to African colonial hospitals. Additionally, I analyze using descriptive statistics the number of inpatients that were attended to at missionary hospitals relative to African colonial hospitals.

In the next step, I analyze the enduring impact of missionary exposure on HIV and related health behaviors in Zambia. To achieve this, I merge the three waves of the Demographic Health Survey, 2007, 2014, 2018–2019. In ArcMap, I draw 30 km buffers around the place of residence for each cluster in the new panel data. I then calculate average values for selected historical-geographical features. I calculate the mean land elevation within each 30 km buffer. Additionally, I calculate the distances from each cluster's residence to the nearest missionary station, missionary health hospital, river, explorer route, and railway line.

Ultimately, I use the Euclidean distance from an individual's residence to the nearest historical missionary station and hospital as proxies for missionary exposure. In this estimation, the main outcome variables are dichotomous variables for HIV status, condom use at first intercourse and pre-marital abstinence, and a continuous variable that captures the individual's age at the first sexual encounter and the number of lifetime partners. In this analysis, I control for selected variables that determined missionary expansion to ameliorate any endogenous bias in the estimations. Furthermore, I also control for provincial and occupational fixed effects. I employ a Probit estimation for models that use dichotomous variables as outcome variables. For models that use continuous variables as outcome variables, I use Ordinary Least Squares (OLS) to estimate the models.

References

Béthune, L. (1889). *Les Missions catholiques d'Afrique*. Desclée, De Brouwer & Cie.

Davies, D. H. (1971). *Zambia in maps*. University of London Press.

Dennis, J., Beach, H., & Fahs, C. (1903). *World Statistics of Christian Missions*. Student Volunteer movement for foreign missions.

Gann, L. H. (1969). *A history of Northern Rhodesia: Early days to 1953*. Humanities Press.

Gelfand, M. (1961). Northern Rhodesia in the days of the Charter. A Medical and Social Study 1878–1924. In *Northern Rhodesia in the days of the Charter. A Medical and Social Study 1878–1924*. B. Blackwell.

Jedwab, R., Meier zu Selhausen, F., & Moradi, A. (2022). The economics of missionary expansion: Evidence from Africa and implications for development. *Journal of Economic Growth, 27*(2), 149–192.

Jenkin, S. (2018). *Foreign investment in agricultural development: The past of the present in Zambia*. Lund University.

Juif, D., & Frankema, E. (2018). From coercion to compensation: Institutional responses to labour scarcity in the Central African Copperbelt. *Journal of Institutional Economics, 14*(2), 313–343.

Kelly, M. J. (1999). *The origins and developments of education in Zambia from Pre-Colonial Time to 1996: A Book of Notes and Readings*. Image Publishers.

Kiszewski, A., Mellinger, A., Spielman, A., Malaney, P., Sachs, S. E., & Sachs, J. (2004). A global index representing the stability of malaria transmission. *The American Journal of Tropical Medicine and Hygiene, 70*(5), 486–498.

Klein Goldewijk, K., Beusen, A., & Janssen, P. (2010). Long-term dynamic modeling of global population and built-up area in a spatially explicit way: HYDE 3.1. *The Holocene, 20*(4), 565–573.
Maina, J., Ouma, P. O., Macharia, P. M., Alegana, V. A., Mitto, B., Fall, I. S., … Okiro, E. A. (2019). A spatial database of health facilities managed by the public health sector in sub-Saharan Africa. *Scientific data, 6*(1), 1–8.
Murdock, G. P. (1967). Ethnographic atlas: A summary. *Ethnology, 6*(2), 109–236.
Nunn, N., & Wantchekon, L. (2011). The slave trade and the origins of mistrust in Africa. *American Economic Review, 101*(7), 3221–3252.
Roome, W. J. W. (1925). *Ethnographic survey of Africa. Showing the tribes and languages; Also the stations of missionary societies*. E. Stanford Limited.
Snelson, P. (1974). Educational development in northern Rhodesia 1883–1945.

6

Results and Discussion

Abstract This chapter unveils the primary outcomes. The study reveals that economic, geographical, and agricultural elements played pivotal roles in shaping the pace of missionary expansion in Zambia. While the progression of missionary education was gradual and unequal between genders during the colonial era. Moreover, medical missionaries notably addressed the healthcare needs of the African populace, leveraging local auxiliaries. Additionally, the evidence underscores that historical exposure to missionaries continues to exert a substantial influence on education and health outcomes in Zambia.

Keywords Long-term development • Christian missionaries • Health

Missionary Expansion

The work of Christian missionaries in the early nineteenth century in Central Africa preceded the Europeans' colonization. Upon arrival in Central Africa, the missionaries first settled in the coastal areas and, after that, they proceeded to explore inland (Gann, 1968). David Livingstone

M. Chanda Chiseni, *The Economic Impact of Christian Missionaries in Zambia*,
https://doi.org/10.1007/978-3-031-65304-9_6

was the earliest Christian missionary to explore Northern Rhodesia; his mission into Northern Rhodesia began from Cape Town, transitioned into Linyanti, and ultimately penetrated Northern Rhodesia via the Zambezi river (Beck, 2007; Rotberg, 1965). The expeditions of David Livingstone in Central Africa paved the way for missionaries that joined the mission field after him (Gann, 1968). Because missionaries established themselves in coastal areas before moving into the interior, distance to the coastline played a vital role in the early phases of missionary settlement. The evidence from this study corroborates the early historical narratives and recent empirical evidence that in the initial phases of exploration, missionaries established themselves in areas along the African coastline (Alpino & Hammersmark, 2021; Gallup et al., 1999; Gann, 1968). The pattern of settlement along coastal areas is even more pronounced in countries with a coastal line; however, since Zambia is a landlocked country, both the empirical evidence and the early settlement pattern show that missionaries first established themselves in regions that border coastal countries, as can be seen from Fig. 6.1.

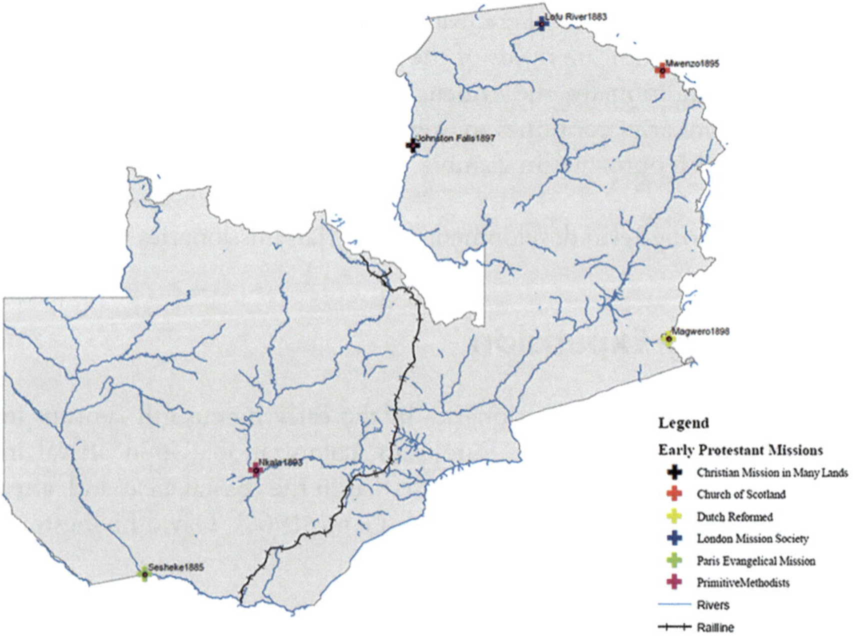

Fig. 6.1 Early protestant missionaries in Northern Rhodesia 1883–1898

As missionaries were moving into the interior, navigable rivers and explorer routes paved by early missionaries and others became important. The evidence in this study shows that missionaries had a predilection for regions near rivers. The rivers were important for transportation, and historically, areas near rivers were more populated and, hence, more likely to develop. The Christian missionaries' evangelistic mission was people-driven; essentially, missionaries sought to establish mission stations in populated regions (Alpino & Hammersmark, 2021; Jedwab et al., 2022; Johnson, 1967).

Additionally, for Northern Rhodesia, before missionaries could establish themselves in any region in Zambia, they needed the approval of the ruling Paramount Chief. The Paramount Chiefs commanded a great influence over the local tribal chiefs; essentially, once the Christian missionaries received the approval of the Paramount Chief, he would then advocate for them to set up mission stations in other chiefdoms under his hegemony (Gann, 1968; Ragsdale, 1986; Snelson, 1974). The findings of this study corroborate this narrative that Chiefs played a pertinent role in facilitating missionary settlement.

Other factors that significantly influenced the settlement of missionaries included the soil fertility and the railway line. Fertile soils made it possible for them to grow various crops for sale and for their livelihood and the railway line enabled missionaries to transport the agricultural produce to the markets. Farming was also used as a proselytization strategy. In 1905, the British South African Company awarded the Jesuit Fathers about 10,000 acres of land in Chikuni among the Tonga people. The land was given to the Jesuits, expecting that the priests would use the land to teach the natives "modern" ploughing methods and make their herds of cattle more productive (Ragsdale, 1986). Essentially, agriculture was therefore an important aspect of the missionaries work in Northern Rhodesia, and many of the missionaries in Northern Rhodesia readily accepted the title "Apostolates of the Plough" (Ragsdale, 1986).

During the period in which this study was conducted, malaria had already been adopted and used in Northern Rhodesia as a prophylactic for malaria. Therefore, the study does not find any evidence that malaria ecology influenced the settlement patterns of missionaries.

Christian Missionaries and Education

The investigation elucidates that gender disparities in Zambia's educational system were significantly shaped by the government's dependence on missionary societies for educational provision. This reliance led to limited advancements in girls' education within government schools, where females constituted less than one-third of the student body. Instead, the majority of girls received their education through missionary societies, which, initially, aimed at providing separate education for girls and boys with a focus on nurturing Christian wives. However, the scarcity of female missionaries posed a substantial hindrance, contributing to the existing gender gap in education, with girls primarily receiving a domesticity-focused curriculum, contrasting with boys who were prepared for colonial economic participation (Snelson, 1974).

Additionally, the findings reveal that educational endeavors during the colonial era predominantly favored boys. In 1925, two-thirds of enrolled students were boys, a trend that continued until the 1940s before gradually reversing (Annual Educational Reports, 1924–1953). This initial gender gap expansion aligns with global patterns of formal education's initial expansion, typically led by boys (Baten et al., 2021). Nevertheless, other studies argue that this bias was intentional, with missionaries directing education toward males, often in collaboration with indigenous elites (Becker & Woessmann, 2008; Boserup, 1970; De Haas & Frankema, 2018). Notably, the study indicates denomination-specific variations in gender access, with Protestant missionary schools in Northern Rhodesia displaying a relatively more equitable distribution than their Catholic counterparts, although the overall gender gap persisted until the end of the colonial period, with 40 percent of girls compared to 60 percent of boys attending school (Annual Educational Report, 1963).

Furthermore, the study identifies a lasting impact of missionary education on educational attainment and the gender gap post-independence. Proximity to a missionary station correlates positively with increased years of education, both for cohorts born during colonial rule and those born post-independence. Despite an overall rise in educational attainment, females consistently lag behind. Girls born in the pre-independence era, on average, received two years less schooling than their male counterparts, though this gap significantly reduced for girls born after independence to half a year on average. While a broader cross-continental study suggests a smaller gender gap in regions intensely exposed to early missionary education (Baten et al., 2021), this study highlights that access to missionary education initially exacerbated the gender gap during the colonial period, possibly due to the educational expansion's strong male bias. Conversely, access to missionary education is associated with a reduced gender gap for cohorts born in Zambia after independence, reflecting increased educational opportunities for girls in the later phases of schooling development.

Christian Missionaries and Health

Establishment of Health Care in Colonial Zambia

As shown in Fig. 6.2, the colonial government operated 12 African hospitals that were mostly situated along the rail line and at their main administrative centers throughout the colonial period. In contrast, in Fig. 6.3 it is noted that missionaries established a larger network of 89 mission hospitals strategically located in rural areas where the majority of Africans lived. This distribution of healthcare facilities reflects the missionaries' focus on establishing hospitals in isolated rural areas, while the state's healthcare provision centered around urban areas. This pattern of missionary dominance in rural healthcare provision, with the state primarily serving urban populations, is not unique to Northern Rhodesia. Similar patterns have been observed in other parts of Africa, such as Malawi (Hokkanen, 2019), Tanganyika (Jennings, 2008; Crozier, 2005), Kenya, and Uganda (Crozier, 2005), particularly in the early years of colonial public health establishment.

The missionaries did not only focus on quantity when establishing healthcare facilities, but rather, the evidence at hand suggests that the majority of missionary hospitals were well-established institutions staffed

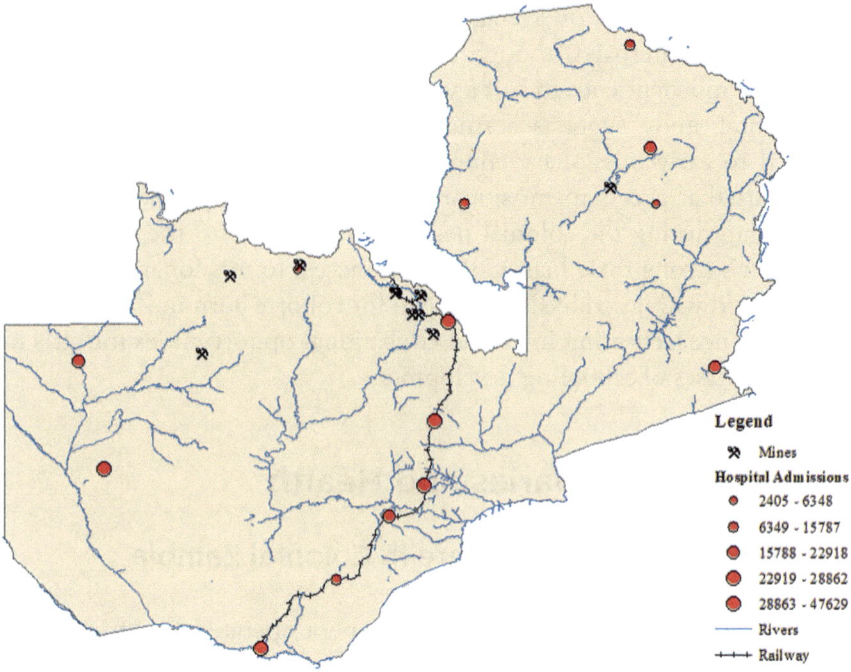

Fig. 6.2 Spatial distribution of government hospitals in Northern Rhodesia 1924–1953. (Source: Drawn by Author)

by qualified medical professionals, enabling them to provide treatment for a wide range of prevalent ailments among the African population. The trust established by the missionaries led to increased visits to missionary healthcare facilities, and the expansion of their services during the colonial period (Gelfand, 1961; Rotberg, 1965). Moreover, the financial support received from the colonial administration and donations from private entities and churches back home played a significant role in facilitating the expansion of missionary medical services.

Figure 6.4 provides a visual representation of the proportion of outpatients who sought medical care at African colonial and missionary hospitals in relation to the total population. According to the data presented in Fig. 6.4, the number of outpatient attendances at missionary hospitals in 1932 initially lagged behind those at African state hospitals. However,

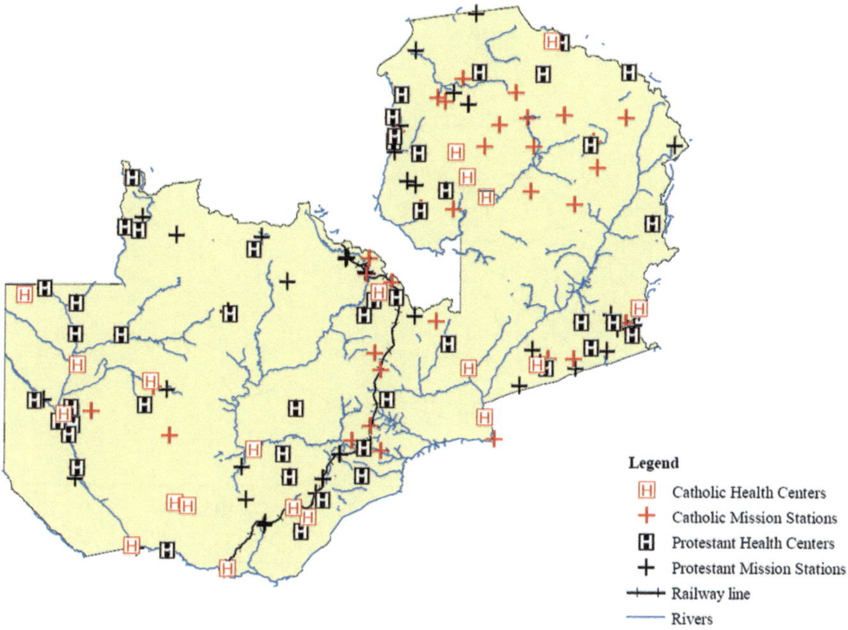

Fig. 6.3 Spatial distribution of missionary hospitals in Northern Rhodesia 1953. (Source: Drawn by Author)

this difference can be attributed to incomplete statistics reported by the missionaries regarding outpatient attendances during that year, as indicated in the colonial medical reports. The evidence presented in Fig. 6.4 suggests that, overall, there were more outpatient attendances at missionary hospitals compared to African state hospitals. Specifically, starting from the 1940s, over 40 percent of the African population sought medical care at missionary hospitals, while less than 20 percent attended African state hospitals as outpatients throughout the colonial period. Missionaries had established themselves as the primary healthcare providers in Northern Rhodesia, with a wide reach, particularly in rural areas. For many Africans residing in rural Northern Rhodesia, missionary healthcare was not only the primary option but often the only available one.

Figure 6.5 illustrates the number of patients who were admitted to government and missionary hospitals in Africa. However, it is important

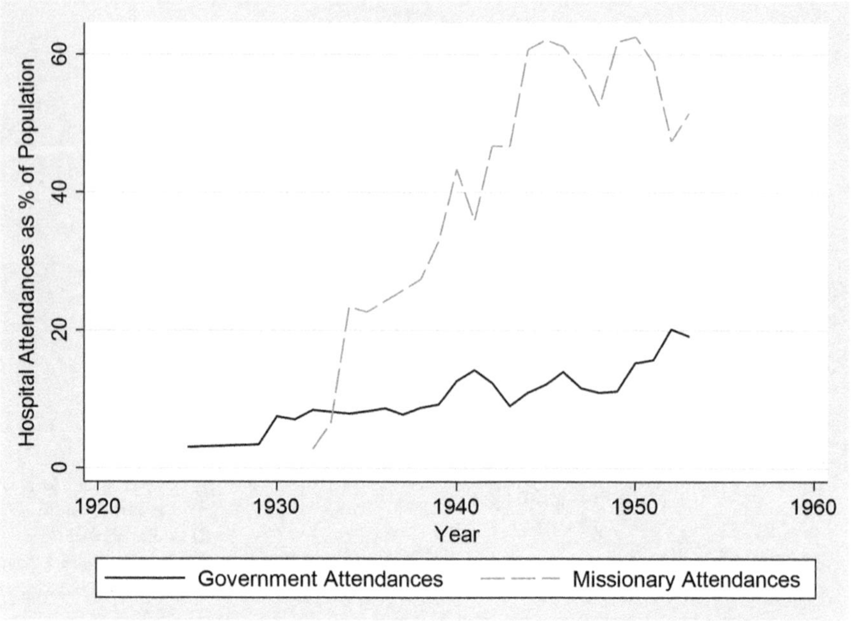

Fig. 6.4 Number of outpatients in government and missionary hospitals as a percentage of the population 1929–1953

to acknowledge that not all missionary hospitals were consistently included in the records of inpatient admissions, and the reporting of these records varied over time, as indicated in the colonial medical reports (Northern Rhodesia Medical Report, 1934, 1939, 1946). Consequently, the data presented in Fig. 6.5 does not offer a comprehensive representation of inpatient admissions in missionary hospitals. Based on the data available in Fig. 6.5, it is evident that there were more inpatient admissions in African government hospitals compared to missionary hospitals. Nevertheless, there is a gradual increase in inpatient admissions in missionary hospitals towards the late 1940s. The sudden surge in inpatient admissions around 1952 could suggest an improvement in the reporting of inpatient admissions from missionary hospitals or a discrepancy in reporting by the colonial government. Throughout the colonial era, the admission rate for Africans in state hospitals remained below 2 percent.

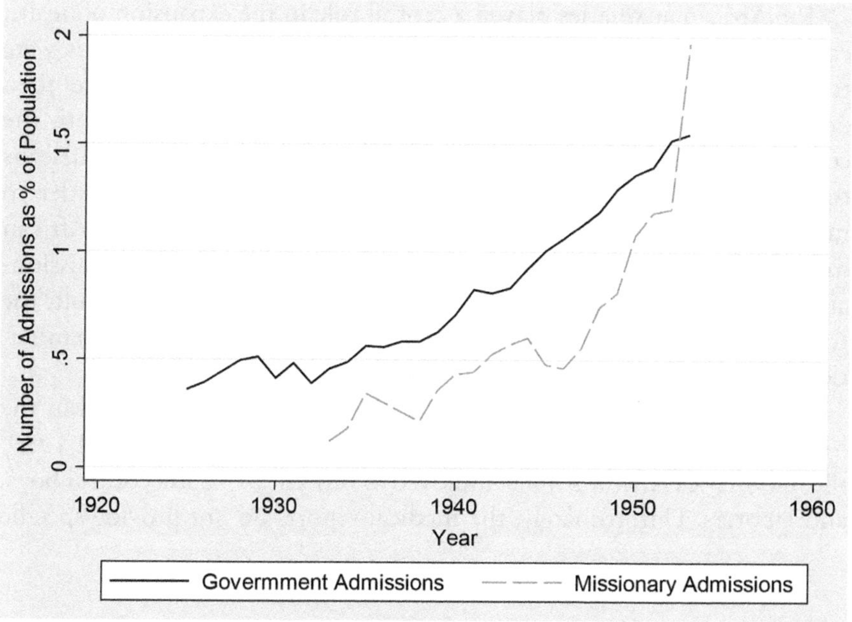

Fig. 6.5 Number of inpatients in government and missionary hospitals as a percentage of the population 1929–1953. (Source: Annual Colonial Medical Reports)

This relatively low rate of admission can be attributed to the limited number of beds available in African state hospitals. For example, according to the colonial blue books, a total of 46 beds were available in six African state hospitals combined in 1925. In 1948, the number of beds in the African state hospitals of Northern Rhodesia had increased to 163, which was spread across seven hospitals out of the total twelve. However, the provision of public healthcare in Northern Rhodesia was deemed insufficient when compared to some other countries in the region. For instance, during the same year, Tanganyika had a significantly higher bed capacity of approximately 3563 beds, which were distributed among 61 African state hospitals, as stated in the Tanganyika Colonial Blue Book of 1948. According to Jennings (2008), by 1963, Tanganyika had further expanded its healthcare infrastructure and boasted over 7000 beds in various state African hospitals.

The African auxiliaries played a central role in the expansion of health care during the era of missionary and colonial rule. These Africans were trained by missionaries in basic medical procedures and were then deployed to work in missionary and colonial state hospitals. Both the colonial state and the missionaries heavily relied on these trained Africans to extend medical services to the Indigenous population. In order to make Western medical practices more acceptable, the trained African medics adapted the medical knowledge they acquired from the missionaries to align with existing Indigenous medical practices. As a result, the trained Africans played a significant role in the expansion and dissemination of missionary medicine.

Figure 6.6 presents a breakdown of the African staff employed in the health sector in Northern Rhodesia. Notably, between 1932 and 1939, the majority of Africans were employed as orderlies, malaria control boys, and laborers. Unfortunately, the medical reports do not provide specific

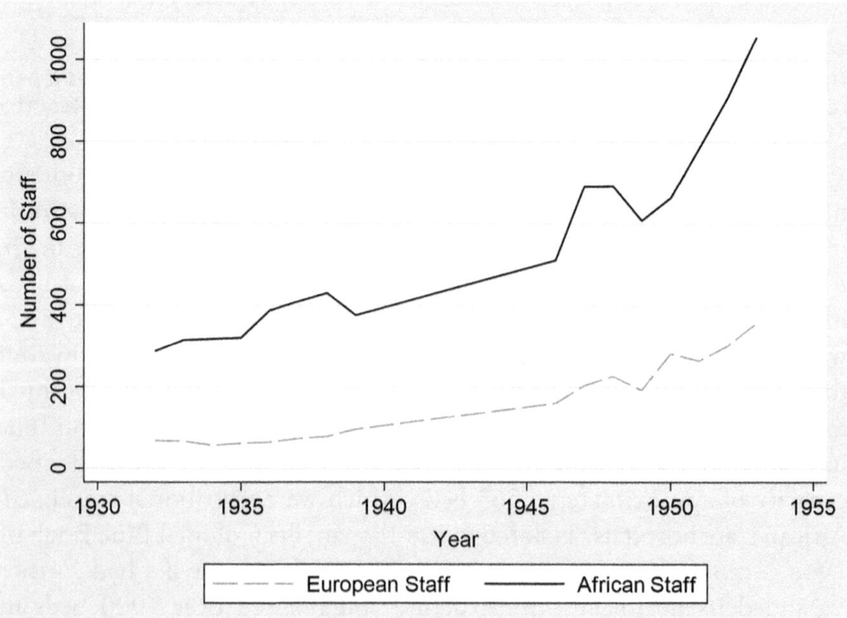

Fig. 6.6 Total number of African and European Staff in Colonial Health Sector Northern Rhodesia 1932–1953. (Source: Annual Colonial Medical Reports)

details about the occupations falling under the category of "other servants." However, it is evident from the reports that a significant number of Africans were employed in missionary hospitals. In 1932, there were 287 Africans employed in government hospitals, and by 1953, this number had increased to 1056, representing a remarkable 267.94 percent increase in African workers in government hospitals alone (Northern Rhodesia Medical Report, 1932, 1953). Africans also constituted the majority of medical staff employed in healthcare in other African countries. For instance, in Kenya, Chaiken (1998) reports that by 1932, approximately one thousand competent African medical staff members were employed in the colonial health sector. Following World War II, Africans held a significant number of mid-level positions.

Christian Missionaries and HIV

This study also delves into the enduring impact of Christian missionaries on HIV prevalence and associated sexual behaviors. The examination of the influence of proximity to historical missionary churches and health centers on HIV infection yields intriguing insights. Notably, regions in close proximity to historical missionary churches exhibit higher HIV infection rates, while the proximity to missionary health centers does not yield a significant impact. This discrepancy in impact can be attributed to the central role of weekly gatherings in missionary churches for inculcating Christian ethos, which potentially explains the pronounced effect observed in relation to missionary churches compared to health centers, many of which continue to serve as places of worship today.

Within the context of HIV prevention, faith-based organizations (FBOs) have actively engaged in combating the disease by advocating Christian doctrines surrounding sexuality. Inspired by the legacy of early missionaries, FBOs promote abstinence before marriage and a lifelong commitment to a single partner. However, it is noteworthy that Christian missionaries generally discourage condom use within their congregations, expressing concerns that discussing condom usage in a church setting might inadvertently encourage sexual promiscuity.

Utilizing proxies for sexual behavior, such as the number of lifetime sex partners, pre-marital abstinence, age at first sex, and condom use at first intercourse, the study scrutinizes individuals residing near missionary churches or health centers. The results unveil a nuanced pattern concerning the impact of proximity to historical missionary churches and health centers on the number of lifetime sex partners. Those residing near historical missionary stations tend to report a higher number of lifetime sex partners compared to their counterparts living at a greater distance, with proximity to a missionary health center showing no significant effect. Further analysis distinguishing between Protestant and Catholic churches indicates that proximity to a Protestant church alone does not significantly influence the number of lifetime sex partners, while proximity to a Catholic church is associated with a higher number of lifetime sex partners, primarily driven by proximity to a Catholic church.

Regarding pre-marital abstinence, individuals living in closer proximity to a historical missionary church are less likely to engage in pre-marital abstinence compared to those residing at a greater distance, with proximity to a missionary health center exhibiting no significant effect. Subsequent analysis based on proximity to Protestant and Catholic churches reveals that this effect is primarily attributed to proximity to a Protestant church, with no significant impact observed for distance to a Catholic church. Individuals residing near a Protestant church are found to be less inclined to practice pre-marital abstinence compared to those living farther away, while no significant impact is detected in proximity to a missionary health center.

The findings further indicate that individuals residing near a historical church tend to initiate sexual activity at an earlier age than those living farther away, primarily driven by proximity to a Protestant church, while no significant impact is detected for distance to a Catholic church. Proximity to a missionary health center does not significantly influence age at first sex. The study does not find any significant impact of proximity to a mission station or health centers on condom usage.

References

Alpino, M., & Hammersmark, E. M. (2021). The role of historical Christian Missions in the location of World Bank Aid in Africa. *The World Bank Economic Review, 35*(1), 207–233.

Annual Educational Report, N. R. (1924). *Northern Rhodesia Native Annual Educational Report.*

Annual Educational Report, N. R. (1925). *Northern Rhodesia Native Annual Educational Report.*

Annual Educational Report, N. R. (1926). *Northern Rhodesia Native Annual Educational Report.*

Annual Educational Report, N. R. (1927). Northern Rhodesia Native Annual Educational Report.

Annual Educational Report, N. R. (1928). Northern Rhodesia Native Annual Educational Report.

Annual Educational Report, N. R. (1929). Northern Rhodesia Native Annual Educational Report.

Annual Educational Report, N. R. (1930). *Northern Rhodesia Native Annual Educational Report.*

Annual Educational Report, N. R. (1931). Northern Rhodesia Native Annual Educational Report.

Annual Educational Report, N. R. (1932). Northern Rhodesia Native Annual Educational Report.

Annual Educational Report, N. R. (1933). Northern Rhodesia Native Annual Educational Report.

Annual Educational Report, N. R. (1934). *Northern Rhodesia Native Annual Educational Report.*

Annual Educational Report, N. R. (1935). Northern Rhodesia Native Annual Educational Report.

Annual Educational Report, N. R. (1936). Northern Rhodesia Native Annual Educational Report.

Annual Educational Report, N. R. (1937). *Northern Rhodesia Native Annual Educational Report.*

Annual Educational Report, N. R. (1938). *Northern Rhodesia Native Annual Educational Report.*

Annual Educational Report, N. R. (1939). *Northern Rhodesia Native Annual Educational Report.*

Annual Educational Report, N. R. (1940). *Northern Rhodesia Native Annual Educational Report.*
Annual Educational Report, N. R. (1941). *Northern Rhodesia Native Annual Educational Report.*
Annual Educational Report, N. R. (1942). *Northern Rhodesia Native Annual Educational Report.*
Annual Educational Report, N. R. (1943). *Northern Rhodesia Native Annual Educational Report.*
Annual Educational Report, N. R. (1944). *Northern Rhodesia Native Annual Educational Report.*
Annual Educational Report, N. R. (1945). *Northern Rhodesia Native Annual Educational Report.*
Annual Educational Report, N. R. (1946). *Northern Rhodesia Native Annual Educational Report.*
Annual Educational Report, N. R. (1947). *Northern Rhodesia Native Annual Educational Report.*
Annual Educational Report, N. R. (1948). *Northern Rhodesia Native Annual Educational Report.*
Annual Educational Report, N. R. (1949). *Northern Rhodesia Native Annual Educational Report.*
Annual Educational Report, N. R. (1950). *Northern Rhodesia Native Annual Educational Report.*
Annual Educational Report, N. R. (1951). *Northern Rhodesia Native Annual Educational Report.*
Annual Educational Report, N. R. (1952). *Northern Rhodesia Native Annual Educational Report.*
Annual Educational Report, N. R. (1953). *Northern Rhodesia Native Annual Educational Report.*
Annual Educational Report, N. R. (1963). *Northern Rhodesia Native Annual Educational Report.*
Baten, J., de Haas, M., Kempter, E., & zu Selhausen, F. M. (2021). Educational gender inequality in Sub-Saharan Africa: A long-term perspective. *Population and Development Review, 47*, 813–849.
Beck, R. B. (2007). All things to all people: Christian missionaries in early Nineteenth-Century South Africa. In *Missions, states, and European expansion in Africa* (pp. 11–34). Routledge.
Becker, S. O., & Woessmann, L. (2008). Luther and the girls: Religious denomination and the female education gap in nineteenth-century Prussia. *Scandinavian Journal of Economics, 110*(4), 777–805.

Boserup, E. (1970). *Woman's role in economic development*. Earthscan.
Chaiken, M. S. (1998). Primary health care initiatives in colonial Kenya. *World development, 26*(9), 1701–1717.
Crozier, A. (2005). *The Colonial Medical Officer and Colonial Identity: Kenya, Uganda and Tanzania Before World War Two*. University of London, University College London (United Kingdom).
De Haas, M., & Frankema, E. (2018). Gender, ethnicity, and unequal opportunity in colonial Uganda: European influences, African realities, and the pitfalls of parish register data. *The Economic History Review, 71*(3), 965–994.
Gallup, J. L., Sachs, J. D., & Mellinger, A. D. (1999). Geography and economic development. *International Regional Science Review, 22*(2), 179–232.
Gann, L. H. (1968). *The birth of a plural society: The development of Northern Rhodesia under the British South Africa Company, 1894–1914*. Manchester University Press.
Gelfand, M. (1961). *Northern Rhodesia in the days of the Charter. A Medical and Social Study 1878–1924*. In *Northern Rhodesia in the days of the Charter. A Medical and Social Study 1878–1924*. B. Blackwell.
Hokkanen, M. (2019). The government medical service and British missions in colonial Malawi, c. 1891–1940: Crucial collaboration, hidden conflicts. In *Beyond the state*. Manchester University Press.
Jedwab, R., Meier zu Selhausen, F., & Moradi, A. (2022). The economics of missionary expansion: Evidence from Africa and implications for development. *Journal of Economic Growth, 27*(2), 149–192.
Jennings, M. (2008). 'Healing of bodies, salvation of souls': Missionary medicine in colonial Tanganyika, 1870s–1939. *Journal of Religion in Africa, 38*(1), 27–56.
Johnson, H. B. (1967). The location of Christian missions in Africa. *Geographical Review, 57*(2), 168–202.
Medical Report, N. R. (1929). *Medical Report on Health and Sanitary Conditions for the Year 1929.*
Medical Report, N. R. (1930). *Medical Report on Health and Sanitary Conditions for the Year 1930.*
Medical Report, N. R. (1931). *Medical Report on Health and Sanitary Conditions for the Year 1931.*
Medical Report, N. R. (1932). *Medical Report on Health and Sanitary Conditions for the Year 1932.*
Medical Report, N. R. (1934). *Medical Report on Health and Sanitary Conditions for the Year 1934.*

Medical Report, N. R. (1935). *Medical Report on Health and Sanitary Conditions for the Year 1935.*
Medical Report, N. R. (1939). *Medical Report on Health and Sanitary Conditions for the Year 1939*
Medical Report, N. R. (1941). *Medical Report on Health and Sanitary Conditions for the Year 1941.*
Medical Report, N. R. (1945). *Medical Report on Health and Sanitary Conditions for the Year 1945.*
Medical Report, N. R. (1946). *Medical Report on Health and Sanitary Conditions for the Year 1946.*
Ragsdale, J. P. (1986). *Protestant mission education in Zambia, 1880–1954.* Susquehanna University Press.
Rotberg, R. I. (1965). *Christian missionaries and the creation of Northern Rhodesia 1880–1924.* Princeton University Press.
Snelson, P. (1974). *Educational development in northern Rhodesia 1883–1945.* Kenneth Kaunda Foundation.

7

Concluding Remarks

Abstract This chapter provides a concise overview of the primary findings presented in the book, which are derived from a comprehensive analysis encompassing four key aspects. These include the factors influencing the selection of missionary locations, the contributions of missionaries in establishing educational institutions and the subsequent long-term effects, the collaborative efforts of both missionaries and Africans in pioneering the colonial healthcare system, and lastly, the influence of Christian missionaries on HIV and associated sexual behaviors in Zambia. Additionally, the chapter highlights potential avenues for further investigation in this field.

Keywords Education • Sub-Saharan Africa • Zambia

While previous literature in the colonial legacies discourse has focused on broader colonial identities and institutional variations, this study takes a novel approach by examining the contributions of Christian missionaries and their investments in human capital as key determinants of long-term development. Specifically, the study focuses on the case of Zambia, a

M. Chanda Chiseni, *The Economic Impact of Christian Missionaries in Zambia*,
https://doi.org/10.1007/978-3-031-65304-9_7

region that experienced a significant influx of missionaries and remains highly Christianized.

In Zambia, the post-independence government made efforts to address the uneven education and health systems inherited from the colonial era, although the country still lags behind in providing adequate human capital development compared to other regions of the world. Furthermore, Zambia has been heavily impacted by the HIV/AIDS epidemic, primarily through heterosexual transmission. Given that missionaries played a pivotal role in education and healthcare provision during the colonial period, studying their impact on current educational attainment and health outcomes in Zambia provides valuable insights.

This study contributes to the existing missionary discourse in several ways. Firstly, it adopts a detailed case study approach, utilizing localized data to highlight the contributions of Christian missionaries in fostering long-run development. Unlike previous studies that rely on single-point references, this research collects new annual colonial and missionary data, enabling a comprehensive understanding of historical development. Additionally, the study combines historical and contemporary data through novel geo-referenced datasets to examine the impact of missionary investments in education and health on present-day outcomes.

Moreover, while qualitative literature on healthcare development in Africa exists, this study stands out as one of the few quantitative studies examining the colonial healthcare system's development in Zambia. By employing a quantitative approach, this research enhances our understanding of the colonial healthcare system's dynamics and sheds light on its historical significance.

The findings of this study emphasize the importance of considering history as a process rather than a single event when analyzing its significance for long-run development. The first paper analyzes the determinants of missionary settlement in Northern Rhodesia, demonstrating that the establishment and expansion of Christian missionaries were deliberate and strategic decisions. Subsequently, the second paper investigates the historical development of formal education in Northern

Rhodesia, highlighting the unparalleled role of missionaries in providing education throughout the colonial period. This research also reveals gender disparities in access to education and shows that historical access to mission education positively influenced long-term educational attainment and reduced the gender gap.

Additionally, this study uses newly collected colonial medical data to establish that missionaries, with the assistance of Africans, pioneered the Western-style healthcare system in Northern Rhodesia and continued to provide the majority of healthcare services during the colonial era. The study further demonstrates successful collaboration between missionaries, African auxiliaries, and the British colonial government in combating epidemic diseases.

Lastly, the study examines the long-term effect of missionary exposure on HIV infection and related sexual behaviors in Zambia. The findings indicate a significant and enduring impact of proximity to historical missionary churches on HIV infection rates, emphasizing the complex relationship between missionary history and contemporary health outcomes.

In summary, this book significantly contributes to our understanding of the long-term impact of historical processes on human capital development. By focusing on the investments of Christian missionaries in education and health, the study uncovers the lasting influence of these investments on Zambia's human capital development. While this study focuses on specific aspects of the long-run impacts of missionaries, the rich Christian historical data presented here lays the groundwork for further exploration of their influence on various other developmental outcomes. One potential area of investigation is the potential impact of Christian missionaries on long-term fertility, as their influence on proselytes' perception of contraceptives may have had an effect. Research has shown that regions with a higher presence of missionaries also experienced greater development in terms of education and healthcare. It would be intriguing to explore whether these regions are now more prosperous compared to areas where missionaries did not establish themselves.

Index[1]

[1] Note: Page numbers followed by 'n' refer to notes.

M. Chanda Chiseni, *The Economic Impact of Christian Missionaries in Zambia*,
https://doi.org/10.1007/978-3-031-65304-9

Printed by Printforce, the Netherlands